400 m/ 0,25 miles

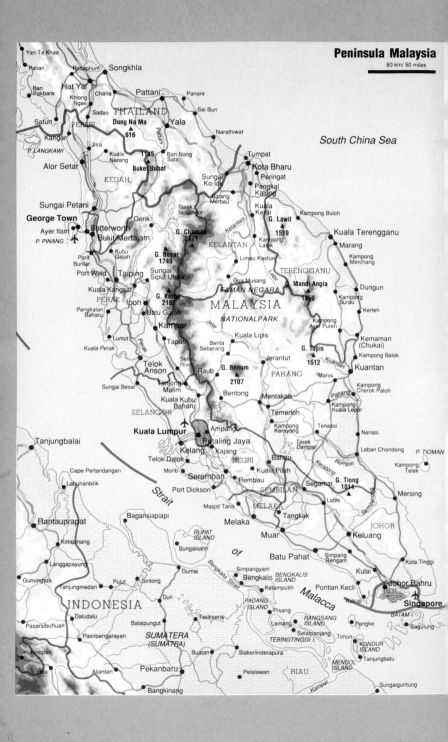

Peninsula Malaysia

80 km/50 miles

South China Sea

Yan Ta Khao
Palian
Ban Pakbara
Rattaphum
Songkhla
Hat Yai
Khlong Ngae
Chana
Pattani
Panare
Sai Buri
THAILAND
Yala
Narathiwat
Satun
Sadao
Dung Na Ma
▲ 616
PERLIS
Kangar
Jitra
Kuala Nerang
Pattani
1145
Ban Nang Sata
Tumpat
P. LANGKAWI
Alor Setar
Buket Bubat
Sungai Ko-lok
Kota Bharu
Peringat
Pangkal Kalong
KEDAH
Gerik
Batang Merbau
Tasek Temenggor
Kuala Krai
Kampong Buloh
Sungai Petani
George Town
Ayer Itam
Butterworth
Bukit Mertajam
G. Chamah
2171 ▲
KELANTAN
Kuala Lalek
G. Lawit
1519 ▲
Kuala Terengganu
P. PINANG
Kubu Gajah
G. Besar
1749 ▲
Limau Kasturi
Marang
Parit Buntar
Port Weld
Taiping
Sungai Siput Utara
Gua Musang
Lebir
TERENGGANU
Kampong Merchang
Kuala Kangsar
PERAK
Ipoh
G. Korbu
2183 ▲
TAMAN NEGARA
G. Mandi Angin
1459 ▲
Dungun
Pengkalan Baharu
Batu Gajah
MALAYSIA
NATIONALPARK
Kampong Surau
Kerteh
Lumut
Kampar
Jelai
Kuala Lipis
Kampong Ayer Puteh
Kemaman
(Chukai)
Kuala Perak
Tapah
Benta Seberang
Jerantut
G. Tapis
1512 ▲
Kuantan
Kampong Balok
Telok Anson
Selim River
Raub
G. Benom
2107 ▲
PAHANG
Manis
Pahang
Kampong Cherok Paloh
Sungai Besar
Tanjong Malim
Bentong
Mentakab
Kampong Kuala Lepar
Kuala Kubu Baharu
SELANGOR
Temerloh
Kampong Kerayong
Tenassi
Nenasi
Kuala Lumpur
Ampang
Petaling Jaya
Tasek Dampar
Leban Chondong
P. TIOMAN
Tanjungbalai
Kelang
Kajang
NEGRI
Bahau
Rompin
Kampong Telek
Telok Datok
Morib
Seremban
Kuala Pilah
Keratong
Port Dickson
Rembau
SEMBILAN
Segamat
G. Tiong
1014 ▲
Mersing
Masjid Tana
MELAKA
Labis
Bagansiapiapi
Tangkak
JOHOR
Melaka
RUPAT ISLAND
Muar
Batu Pahat
Keluang
Rantauprapat
Sungaisahir
of
Simpang Rengam
Kulai
Kota Tinggi
Kotapinang
Dumai
Simpangyam
Bengkalis
Pontian Kecil
Langgapayung
Pujut
Sintong
Duri
Ketamputih
BENGKALIS ISLAND
Johor Bahru
Gunungtua
Tanjungmedan
Malacca
Kukup
Singapore
INDONESIA
Daludalu
Tasikserai
PADANG ISLAND
Pisang
RANGSANG ISLAND
Pangke
BATAM I.
Sagulung
Pasarsibuhuan
Balaipungut
SUMATERA
(SUMATRA)
Pasirpengarayan
Lemang
Selatpanjang
Timun
TEBINGTINGGI I.
KUNDUR ISLAND
Tanjungbatu
Hutanopan
Buatan
Siaksriinderapura
MENDOL ISLAND
Bau
Aliantan
Pekanbaru
Pelalawan
RIAU
Sungaiguntung
Bangkinang
Kampar

Penang

Written and Presented by **Fong Pheng Khuan**

INSIGHT
pocket
GUIDES

Insight Pocket Guide:

PENANG

Directed by
Hans Höfer

Photography by
Ingo Jezierski

Design Concept by
V. Barl

Design by
Karen Hoisington

© 1994 APA Publications (HK) Ltd

All Rights Reserved

Printed in Singapore by
Höfer Press (Pte) Ltd
Fax: 65-8616438

Distributed in the United States by
Houghton Mifflin Company
222 Berkeley Street
Boston, Massachusetts 02116-3764
ISBN: 0-395-69030-7

Distributed in Canada by
Thomas Allen & Son
390 Steelcase Road East
Markham, Ontario L3R 1G2
ISBN: 0-395-69030-7

Distributed in the UK & Ireland by
GeoCenter International UK Ltd
The Viables Center, Harrow Way
Basingstoke, Hampshire RG22 4BJ
ISBN: 9-62421-525-1

Worldwide distribution enquiries:
Höfer Communications Pte Ltd
38 Joo Koon Road
Singapore 2262
ISBN: 9-62421-525-1

Selamat Datang!

Fong Peng Khuan

Whenever I return to Penang, I am reminded of the sleepy *kampung* that I grew up in 30 years ago. The skyline may be taller, the traffic busier and the air not as clean, but some things have not changed. Life is still conducted at a leisurely pace, and people smile readily. There is none of the 'big city' syndrome, no sense of urban paranoia, no devil-may-care attitude among its folks — features that make Penang pleasant, refreshing and endearing, at least for me.

Steer away from the frenzy of organised coach tours and I will lead you on a discovery of the very heart of Penang. The full-day itineraries in this book explore the capital of George Town, with its quaint landmarks and interesting backlanes where surprises abound. There is also an exploratory tour of the northern coast, punctuated with sandy bays, beaches and five-star resorts.

The *Pick and Mix* options are a series of half-day tours for you to combine as you please. Breakfast on piping-hot noodles; weave through morning markets and ethnic enclaves; peek into history at Fort Cornwallis; or ramble through jungle paths in search of rare flora. A *Day Trips* section suggests additional forays around Penang, like scenic Ayer Itam and Penang Hill, and also further afield to Butterworth and Bukit Mertajam on mainland Malaysia.

And of course, you simply cannot leave this island without sampling her varied shopping and food. I've scoured the entire island for the finest food haunts, from simple roadside vendors to posh eateries at resorts. Antique hunters too will find Penang a treasure trove of genuine antiques and excellent 'repros'. This guide is intended as a catalyst, not an iron-bound bible. Wander off the itineraries if you wish when you stumble upon beckoning byways and who knows, you may discover some new secrets for yourself. *Selamat Datang — Welcome!*

Contents

Preceding pages:
Penang Bridge at dawn

Maps

Following pages: decorative tiles
from a Penang house facade

9

Throughout history, Penang has changed names like the seasons. Early Malays called it Pulau Ka Satu, or Single Island. Later, it appeared on sailing charts as Pulau Pinang, or Island of the Betel Nut Tree. Penang was discovered by the Portuguese, the first Europeans to sail into its waters, in the 15th century. Once a pirate's hideout, Penang's position in the Straits of Malacca made it a choice port of call.

The profitable spice trade which spurred the British during the 17th century brought Francis Light, a naval captain who negotiated for it from the Sultan of Kedah, 'as long as the Sun and Moon endure', in return for protection and compensation.

The British found about 100 natives living in Penang when they landed to raise the Union Jack on 11 August 1786. As it was the eve of the British crown prince's birthday, it was christened Prince of Wales Island, but the name never gained popularity.

The settlement that arose was called George Town, after the reigning monarch of England, King George III. This British foothold in Southeast Asia enjoyed a successful growth as an entrepot harbour and station for refueling, supplies and victuals. Its importance, however, was overshadowed when Stamford Raffles, who was first assigned to Penang, acquired and opened up Singapore in 1819.

The Present: City and State

More than 200 years after its founding, Penang has undergone many changes. George Town gained its city status, conferred by Queen Elizabeth II, in 1957. Since then, it has industrialised and developed rapidly. When its historic free port status was lifted, several free trade zones were started to induce foreign companies to invest capital and expertise. The state economy is now sustained by microchip and hi-tech industries.

A popular port of call for cruisers, ships and airplanes, Penang's tourist traffic has picked up with the proliferation of hotels. No matter if it is a bit off the well-trodden route. Travellers, be they backpackers or well-heeled individuals, like what they find here.

Landmarks: Port, Tower and Hill

The port area is the oldest part of the city. There are many recorded references to it in books. The best way to orientate yourself is to start from the port area as most places of historic interest

are found in its neighbourhood. Walking tours are recommended to explore its nooks and crannies, side streets and alleyways.

KOMTAR is the 65-storey podium complex in the heart of George Town. The viewing gallery on the 58th floor enables visitors to see the whole city. At street level below the high tower are local public bus and taxi terminals.

Penang Hill offers vantage points to survey the island. On a clear day, you can see for miles around from its summit. It is also a nice spot for a panoramic view of the city at night when it becomes bejewelled with lights.

People: Melting Pot Syndrome

Penang is mini-Asia in a nutshell. This cosmopolitan place was born as an ancient crossroads of traders from many corners of the world. Arabs brought Islam and perfumes from the Middle East; Europeans introduced western science and philosophy; Indians came with opium and cottons; Chinese merchants arrived with tea, silk and porcelain; nearby islanders bartered spices and food.

It has resulted in a society of many faceted cultures where different religions abound. The diverse and contrasting ways of life somehow complement each other. A blend of peoples and tongues of many nations has forged an integrated and interesting society.

George Town, with Penang Bridge in the background

Historical Highlights

1400 Evidence of Malayan Stone Age found 3–5m (10–15ft) below ground on 18 December 1965 at Bukit Gambir, Glugor.

1405 Admiral Cheng Ho visited Malacca using Chinese charts on which Penang is mentioned.

1592 James Lancaster, an Elizabethan captain, called at Penang and reported about its good harbour back in England.

1599 Hakluyt's map of Southeast Asia listed Penang as Pulo Pinaom in the second volume of *Navigations and Discoveries* published that year.

1765 The India-based British trading company of Jourdain, Sullivan & de Souza sent Francis Light to explore and establish mercantile ties in the Straits of Malacca.

1784 Light began negotiations with Sultan Abdullah of Kedah to start a settlement in Penang.

1786 The British landed with a garrison of troops from three ships and took over Penang on 11 August and the Union Jack was raised.

1790 Sultan Abdullah prepared to seize Penang from the British with whom he was disillusioned.

1791 Light's men raided the invading forces at camp by night and forced the sultan to seek peace.

1792 The population had increased to 10,000 people. Many were lured by business opportunities and the chance to seek fortunes.

1794 Capt Light died of malaria.

1800 A strip of land opposite the island was ceded by the Kedah sultanate under a new treaty. It was renamed Province Wellesley after the Governor General of India then.

1804 Penang was upgraded to a presidency from a mere settlement.

1805 Stamford Raffles arrived to serve in Penang as an official of the East India Company. He was assistant secretary to Philip Dundas, the new governor of Penang.

1816 Penang Free School started, marking the importance of education for the people.

1832 Penang became the capital of the newly-formed Straits Settlements, comprising Malacca and Singapore as well.

1835 Singapore replaced Penang as capital of the Straits Settlements.

1867 Penang, Malacca and Singapore were declared British Crown Colonies.

1888 George Town became a municipality.

1905 Electric power came to Penang when a hydro-electric scheme was successfully completed. The first electric tramway was introduced a year later.

1910 The automobile industry sparked a boom in the rubber trade and Penang enjoyed growth as an export centre and port.

1914 World War I spurred the demand for tin and rubber and Penang thrived as a major collection and distribution point.

1923 Completion of the Penang Hill railway.

1929 The Great Depression.

1941–45 Japanese Occupation of Malaya during World War II.

1945 The Japanese surrendered on 4 September.

1948 Penang joined the Federation of Malaya.

1957 George Town conferred city status on 1 Jan. Independence declared for the country on 31 Aug.

1963 Malaysia was formed comprising the Malay Peninsula, Singapore, Sabah and Sarawak.

1965 Singapore left the federation to become an independent nation.

1970 Tun Abdul Razak took over from Tunku Abdul Rahman as Malaysia's second Prime Minister.

1975 Tun Hussein Onn became Prime Minister when Tun Razak died.

1981 Datuk Seri Dr Mahathir Mohamad was elected Malaysia's fourth Prime Minister.

1985 The 13½-km (8½-mile) Penang Bridge opened to traffic on 1 Sep.

1986 Bicentennial of Penang's founding.

Day Itiner

Spend a few days in Penang. You will discover that city life isn't only what this bustling island offers. Penangites will endear you to them with their ready smiles and their spontaneity. So though these itineraries will guide you around, venture further if you wish: you won't have to look far for a friendly local willing to give you directions.

Day ①

City Sights

Wander through the city centre. Lunch at the KOMTAR, getting your bearings right from the start.

Once the Main Street of the city, **Penang Road** retains a faded charm even though it is no longer bustling like it used to 20 years ago. For your first day, this is the place to savour a real slice of daily life in George Town.

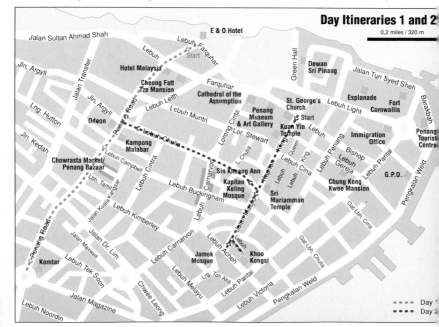

Day Itineraries 1 and 2

0,2 miles / 320 m

- • • • Day
- • • • Day 2

ries

Start your walk opposite the **E & O Hotel** (short for 'Eastern and Oriental') standing by the waterfront. The hotel was built in 1885 by the Sarkies brothers, enterprising Armenians who also developed the legendary Raffles Hotel in Singapore.

This 'dowager of Penang hotels' once hosted visiting dignitaries and famous guests like Somerset

Ready to start exploring from the E & O Hotel

Maugham and Mary Pickford. The ballroom is now closed although a sun terrace, bar and restaurant still attract patrons.

Directly across the street from the E & O is the Esso Station. It marks the beginning of Penang Road. Head left from the station past a row of antiquated shophouses which offer browsers much to look at (see *Shopping*). Keep walking till you see **Hot Lips** pub lying at the junction of Penang Road and Lebuh Farquhar. To continue on Penang Road, cross Lebuh Farquhar and you will get to **Hotel Malaysia**, which is at the start of a stretch of tourist hotels, shops and restaurants. This area seems innocent enough by day, but comes alive after nightfall when discos, cocktail lounges and social escort agencies open for business.

By way of contrast, the **Catholic Information Centre** outside the St Francis Xavier Church and orphanage has rosaries, holy pictures and prayer books for the religious.

Breakfast at the Kedai Kopi Kheng Pin

Keep walking down Penang Road. About 300m (340yds) from Hotel Malaysia is a good breakfast spot, the **Kedai Kopi Kheng Pin**, at the corner of Jalan Sri Bahari on the right. Locals frequent it for the chicken rice, satay and noodles which are served on round mat-

KOMTAR Tower and old houses

ble top tables. Hot drinks are made instantly after your order. For more expensive and exotic fare, there is a choice of North Indian, Chinese, Japanese and seafood restaurants in the same vicinity. Taxis stop and pick passengers outside these restaurants as this is one of their rest stations.

About 50m (54½yds) to the right of Kedai Kopi Kheng Pin, the **Odeon cinema** lies at the four-way junction with Lebuh Chulia, (which has many shoestring hotels), Lebuh Leith and Jalan Argyll. Before you reach it, there are more shops including a travel agency, tailor, camera dealer and optician.

The **Odeon** offers a mix of English, Chinese and Malay movies, screened during afternoons and evenings. From the Odeon, proceed for another 500m (545yds) toward the traffic lights till you reach Lebuh Campbell and Hutton Lane junctions. There you see the

Candy stall

Cathay Cinema, which faces the **Penang Bazaar**, a congested area full of small stalls selling textiles, clothes, bags and a million other things. Exploring the bazaar can be amusing as you watch vendors compete with one another for your attention.

Just past Penang Bazaar on the left is the **Chowrasta Market** which lies opposite the city police headquarters, a big white building with its entrance at Lebuh Dickens.

After bazaar browsing, continue down Penang Road towards the traffic light junction near the Capitol cinema. Use the pedestrian crossing as traffic is heavy here. On the way, you see more shops on either side of the busy one-way road.

Look out for a popular lunch spot on the right – the busy, congested **Kek Seng** coffeeshop opposite Singapore Hotel at No. 382-384 Jalan Penang. You might like to have lunch later here. Be warned though; the coffeeshop is packed with office workers during mid-day. Stand around and wait for a table to be available, or ask to share one with other lunchers. Almost every foodstall here is good. You won't go wrong if you order something that catches your eye. For under RM5 per person, you can have a feast to last till dinner. The corn and durian ice-cream with or without *ais kachang* makes a great dessert after a meal of tasty noodles. This coffeeshop opens from 9am till midnight.

Continue beyond the shophouses to the tall **Kompleks Tun Abdul Razak** (KOMTAR for short) on the left. The most conspicuous structure of this complex is the 65-story KOMTAR tower, a huge sprawling building with many entrances. The building contains many civic and administrative offices.

On the 58th level of the KOMTAR tower is the **Tower Tourist Centre** (TTC), a com-

Proud owner of the Jaguar

mercialised observation deck. Buy an entry ticket for RM5 into the TTC from the Tourist Information Centre on the 3rd floor of KOMTAR, located beside the entrance to the Government offices. You will then be escorted to a non-stop lift which will take you to the TTC. Keep your admission ticket as it is redeemable against food and beverage bills incurred at outlets within the TTC.

The TTC on the 58th floor which opens from 10am to 10pm has a grand viewing gallery that runs around the whole floor. From here, you have a panorama of rooftops, houses and the harbour in the distance. Penang native products, batik, souvenirs, handicrafts and other items are on sale and you can pose for photographs in a trishaw.

A floor above, on the 59th level, you will find **Tower Palace** Chinese restaurant and coffee lounge. A daily buffet lunch, high tea and buffet dinner are available. A *karaoke* club on the 60th floor is open from 8.30pm till 1am nightly, in case you feel like straining your vocal chords later. There are furnished suites available for official or private functions. Call 622-222/633 for more information.

The international class hotel, **Shangri-La**, which is part of the KOMTAR complex, has its entrance at Jalan Magazine right behind the KOMTAR tower, the geodesic dome, and Yaohan department store. The hotel features several restaurants, conference rooms, a banquet hall, fitness and business centres and other modern facilities. The **Shang Palace** on the first floor serves delicious but pricey *dim sum* for breakfast and lunch. Businessmen frequent the restaurant when entertaining clients so you are advised to make reservations if you plan to lunch here.

KOMTAR has a labyrinthian warren of boutiques, fast food outlets, amusement centres, restaurants and shops. There are two major department stores, **Yaohan** and **Super Komtar**, which stock food, household goods, garments, cosmetics, electronics and sporting goods.

Shop in air-conditioned comfort and if you get hungry while doing so and don't wish to leave the KOMTAR building, catch a quick bite at any one of the fast food joints. However, it is preferable that you leave the complex and head for the Kek Seng coffeeshop mentioned earlier, for typical Penang food and a convivial coffeeshop atmosphere.

Altogether, over 300 retail establishments abound, though most are small, specialising in jewellery, fashion, video and other consumer items. This one-stop shopping mall is a popular haunt with the local people. It will be late afternoon when you have paced the length of Jalan Penang and its surroundings.

You can catch a yellow top taxicab from the station near the grand outdoor staircase of KOMTAR on the side of the complex facing **Jalan Dr Lim Chwee Leong** or catch the municipal buses from the bus-stop below the Dalit Cinema and near the ground level entrance of Yaohan Department Store.

Another convenient taxi stand for a ride back to your hotel is at **Jade Auto**, 25 Jalan Burmah (Tel: 373-015), open 24 hours. You can reserve a cab to take you out the next day or to meet you at an appointed place.

When travelling about town, remember that the taxis charge a minimum of RM4 even for a short distance. Though the cabs have meters, these are never used, so settle on a fixed price to your destination before hiring them.

Indian jewellery shop, Penang Road

Day (2)

Secrets of George Town

Take in the temples and mosques in and around Jalan Masjid Kapitan Keling; lunch at Sin Kheang Aun; tour Lebuh Chulia; have dinner at Kampung Malabar.

Alleys, hidden passages and paths worth exploring are in the oldest quarter of George Town. In particular, the **Jalan Masjid Kapitan Keling** (formerly Pitt Street) area has a wealth of sights and buildings like churches, mosques and temples. They attest to religious freedom and reveal the city's mixture of cultures and ethnic backgrounds. Some dub this 'the street of harmony' because of the many houses of different religious faiths represented along the same street.

St. George's Church

Tell the taxi driver to drop you at the imposing **St George's Church**, the oldest Anglican house of worship in the region. Opposite is the High Court Building. Begin your walking tour from the church. Preserved almost intact, this landmark was built with the labour of convicts in 1817. The roof used to be flat but was redone to the present gable form after suf-

Kuan Yin Teng Temple, figurine

fering damage during the Allied Forces' bombing of George Town in 1945. In its present form, it has a lofty spire and the facade shows a Doric portico with huge white columns rising from a marble floor. A memorial to Captain Francis Light stands on its front lawn.

About 150m (545yds) behind the church is the modern, high-rise Chinese Town Hall which is often used for exhibitions, talks and seminars.

Next door to the right is the **Kuan Yin Teng**, the Goddess of Mercy Temple. Built in 1800 by early immigrant settlers from China, it faces the Lebuh Cina junction. Businessmen flock to the temple almost daily. On the first and 15th day of the Chinese lunar calendar month, devotees crowd its interior to pray and burn joss paper and candles.

The four guardian dragons on its red roof are not as visible as the pair of stone sculptured lions in the front courtyard laid with granite blocks for heavy duty walking. Puppet and opera shows are often held there in full view of passers-by. Outside the temple are florists and joss and incense vendors. During major festivals, pilgrims outnumber the pigeons which flock there throughout the year. Three annual anniversaries of Kuan Yin are observed by her followers: the 19th days of the second, sixth and ninth moons which are her birthday and the days she became a nun and attained enlightenment respectively.

Sri Mariamman Temple

Kapitan Keling Mosque

Across the road on the left is a row of money changers and jewellery shops. After that is **Sri Maha Mariamman**, the oldest Hindu temple in Penang, built in 1883. It is dedicated to Lord Subramaniam whose gem-encrusted statue is paraded annually during the Thaipusam festival. Hindu gods and goddesses are sculptured above its locked doorway at the temple which faces Jalan Masjid Kapitan Keling. The main entrance to Sri Maha Mariamman is at Lebuh Queen, the street parallel to and behind Jalan Masjid Kapitan Keling about 100m (110yds) to the left. Ask for permission to enter. Early morning or late afternoon is the best time to see people at prayer and the priest performing rituals.

Some 300m (330yds) down the road on the right is the Moorish-style **Kapitan Keling Mosque** adjacent to Lebuh Buckingham. The present building which features domes, turrets and minarets is on the site of an earlier mosque constructed around 1800 by Cauder Mohideen, the then Indian Muslim leader.

Its exterior is ochre yellow; inside, the white marble floor is cool and the ceilings high. Prayer time is announced over a loudspeaker in the tall tower on the grounds. A *nasi kandar* stall in the tiny alley beside the mosque does a thriving business dishing out curry meals for breakfast, lunch and dinner.

About 100m (110yds) diagonally to the right is Lebuh Cannon, at the end of which stands the old **Jamek Mosque** built in 1808 on Lebuh Acheh. It was built on land donated by a rich Muslim merchant. The round window in the Egyptian-style minaret was made by a cannon-ball during civil disturbances by feuding secret societies in 1867. Entry should be approved by mosque officials. Visitors wearing shorts or with bare shoulders are not allowed inside this and other mosques.

Double back to Lebuh Cannon from Lebuh Acheh. There are 20 Chinese temples and clan houses in George Town but the **Khoo**

Kongsi at Cannon Square is the most ornate. Gain access via a lane on the right side of Lebuh Cannon. The alley is lined with houses with their porch walls embellished with red and gold shrines. Round the corner is a gilded marvel. Observe the temple's spread-eagled roof, massive columns, carved ceiling, frescoed walls, bas-reliefs, friezes and opulent halls. A theatre-stage for live opera shows lies across the granite paved courtyard. Entry is permitted by the temple office, open weekdays from 9am to 5pm, and Saturdays from 9am to 1pm.

The temple's outstanding architecture, dating from 1906, is worth a snapshot or two. Besides the main Dragon Mountain Hall are two other rooms dedicated to the Khoo ancestors and the Chinese god of prosperity. The complex in which the temple is sited has three entrances. The formal entrance is at Lebuh Pantai. Another way is through the Lebuh Armenian passage. But you want to back out to **Lebuh Cannon**.

For lunch, walk back towards the Kapitan Keling mosque and head in the direction of the traffic lights on the pedestrian walkway which usually has pigeons perched on it. Turn left onto **Lebuh**

Swiss Hotel –
for the budget traveller

Chulia where you see the Eu Yen Sang medicinal shop. Go up the street along the covered corridor of the shophouses. Some 200m (220yds) away on the right is **Sin Kheang Aun** at No. 2 Lorong Chulia which is 50m (54½yds) from the road junction.

This small and compact restaurant serves *Hailam* cuisine for lunch and dinner. Reservations are preferred (Tel: 614-786). The house specialities include *curry chicken kapitan*, shrimp salad (*kerabu*), duck with yam soup, *curry fish tumis*, *asam* prawns and bean sprouts with salted fish. Go upstairs if the ground level is fully occupied. A dumb waiter conveys food to diners on the first floor. Opening hours are from 11am to 2.30pm and 5pm to 8pm.

After a hearty repast, return to Lebuh Chulia. This is the street made famous by backpackers and budget travellers. Some of the budget hotels are visible from the street while others are hidden from sight behind the two rows of shophouses.

The most popular are Swiss Hotel at No. 431 Lebuh Chulia and Eng Aun Hotel opposite it. Though basic, they are kept clean and tidy. Similar but smaller inns are Tye Ann at No. 282 Lebuh Chulia, Yee Hing at No. 302, Yeng Keng at No. 362, Nam Wah at No. 381, Chung King at No. 398 and Eastern at No. 509. The inns are accustomed to having foreigners and are usually adept at preparing western food like baked beans on toast, omelettes, sausages and burgers.

When approached by touts selling bus, rail and air tickets to Singapore, Thailand and Indonesia, be on your guard and insist on receipts. These are issued at any licensed travel agency legitimately registered with the Malaysian government. Do not take unnecessary risks by leaving your passport behind or paying a hefty deposit before collecting your ticket, no matter how good the bargain. While in public areas such as a coffeeshop or in the street, watch out for over-friendly strangers. Lebuh Chulia has its fair share of locals and foreigners who hustle and prey on unsuspecting tourists.

Towards the end of Lebuh Chulia are shops specialising in rattan and

Khoo Kongsi Temple

Lebuh Chulia rattanware

basket wares, souvenirs and used books. Browse around for a cane walking stick, a carving or whatever strikes your fancy. The second-hand bookstores carry a wide range of titles and you can trade old books with the store keeper. If you do not wish to buy a book but prefer to peruse it at leisure, you can pay a deposit and get a partial refund upon returning it after reading.

As the day turns to dusk, you will have explored the whole length of not only Jalan Masjid Kapitan Keling in the morning, but Lebuh Chulia in the afternoon as well. If you are exhausted by this time, you might wish to return to your hotel for rest before dinner. If not, you can have an early dinner at **Kampong Malabar**, a hawker rendezvous located less than 200m (220yds) to the left of the traffic lights at the corner of Lebuh Chulia with Penang Road. If you are staying at a hotel nearby, you could return to this spot after a short rest for a hearty meal.

Here, you will find a selection of coffeeshops offering local favourites such as *lobak* or pork roll, pork porridge, dim sum, curry noodles, roast and barbecued pork with rice and beef balls.

Sun and Fun

Sunbathe and swim at either Tanjung Bungah, Batu Ferringhi or Teluk Bahang beaches. Lunch at Hollywood Restaurant or Sin Hai Kheng in Tanjung Bungah; on to Craft Batik and the butterfly farm; dinner and cultural show at Eden Seafood Village in Batu Ferringhi.

Sun, sand and sea fun in the tourist belt of the north coast is Penang's claim to resort fame. Luxury hotels are havens of calm amidst the action and hustle outside, where vendors and shops abound.

Daytripping is suggested for town hotel dwellers. No visit to Penang is complete without a visit to its fine-powdered public beaches. Enjoyable as it may be to spend a day soaking in the sun while feasting from a picnic basket, do be warned, Islam, the main religion in Malaysia; forbids nudity in public, so skinny dipping is out. Some of the locals are so conservative that they even swim fully clothed. There are lots of bays and coves which are frequently deserted. Enjoy yourself in any of them. Remember to keep an eye on your belongings; never swim too far out in case they get pilfered.

Batu Ferringhi Beach

The waters are safe, no sharks! However, the strong undercurrents are dangerous, so be careful if you are not a good swimmer. The jellyfish menace surfaces now and again when too many float to the surface and get in the way of swimmers. Avoid globs of translucent matter bobbing in the sea as these may be jellyfish with trailing tentacles which sting when they sweep over your body. If that happens, you should overcome prejudices and pour human urine over the affected area immediately, then seek medical attention.

On the off chance that a sea snake bites, try to get a good look at the culprit to identify its colour, size and length. There are effective serums to counteract its venom at the Snake Research Institute at the general hospital in Penang. Go there immediately for treatment.

Generally, the picture of Penang as a sun-drenched island with coconut palms fringing its shores still endures. Some beaches are rocky and may even resemble Zen rock gardens but those in the prime resort areas of Batu Ferringhi and Teluk Bahang are long, sweeping curves of uncluttered, sandy beach.

To get to the northern stretch of coastal beaches from George Town, either catch a cab or hire a car. It the latter is your option, here are the directions: when you get off the ferry, take the road at **Pengkalan Weld**, turn right and then left to the roundabout in front of the Clock Tower. Take a semi-circular turn at the roundabout and you are now in Lebuh Light which connects with Lebuh Farquhar.

Continue until you pass Jalan Sultan Ahmad Shah with its palatial residences. At the roundabout, make a semi-circular turn to get on Jalan Kelawei, which has shady trees all the way, until another roundabout with ornamental palms appears. To its right is Sunrise supermarket with a McDonald's on the ground floor.

Make another semi-circular turn and

Waterskiing at Ferringhi

you will be on **Tanjung Tokong**, flanked by vegetable gardens with a fire station on the left. From Tanjung Tokong onwards, the sea is always on your right. Just follow this main road all the way as it links up with **Tanjung Bungah** which in turn becomes **Batu Ferringhi** and **Teluk Bahang**.

Pick your beach spots. You may even want to go from one beach to another, if you wish. Whatever the case, you will want to head towards **Teluk Bahang** later to visit the **Craft Batik factory**, **Butterfly Farm**, **Orchid Farm** and the **Forestry Museum**.

Tanjung Bungah, the Cape of Flowers, begins near **Motel Sri Pantai** and the **Chinese Swimming Club**, which has some inexpensive rooms, a restaurant and an Olympic-size pool. About 300m (330yds) up the road on the right is **Park Inn**, followed by the **Penang Swimming Club**, the **Novotel Penang,** which has its own secluded stretch of beach, and the **Crown Prince Hotel**. These are opposite the Hillside residential area and just before the Dalat School (formerly called Sandycroft), a private high school with an American curriculum for expatriate kids.

About 300m (330yds) away is the Ocean Hotel and Sauna House, standing side by side, which have massage parlours and bars. Further up is the post office and police station which are opposite each other and the **Tanjung Bungah bus station** in Jalan Chan Siew Teong (Chee Seng Garden). Nearby on the main road are a cluster of coffeeshops, restaurants and foodstalls. Have a quick snack from the *goreng pisang* (banana fritters) pushcart located out-

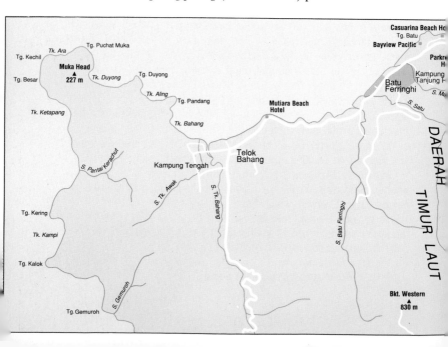

side Restoran Bahagia
and Thean Ai Tong Medical Hall
& General Goods.

The **Asian Pottery** shop has lots of modern
ceramic wares for sale. Two popular restaurants on
this stretch are **New Seaview Seafood Village** (Sin Hai Keng)
and **Hollywood**. Some 100m (110yds) away is the **Mar Vista
Resort**, a condominium complex built on a ridge at the end of this
stretch and situated opposite the beachfront mosque, Masjid Jamek
Tanjung Bungah.

Once past Mar Vista Resort, it is **Batu Ferringhi** and the first
beach, **Sunshine**, beside the Lost Paradise Guesthouse and Boon
Siew Villa on the right. The next picnic beach is **Shamrock**, which
faces the modest Seaview Hotel and Restaurant on the left and the
Mount Pleasure condominiums. Several road bends later are Ferringhi Beach Hotel and the Pantai Miami residential site on the left
side of the road. They overlook **Miami Beach**, a sandy expanse with
a lifeguard lookout on the shore.

Continue going past the secluded **Moonlight Bay** which is found

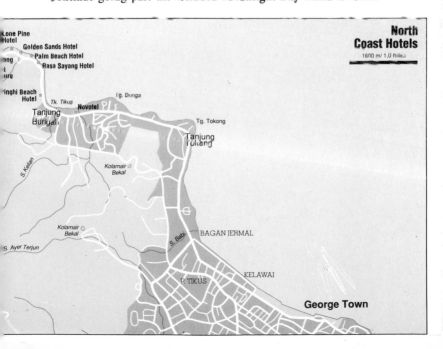

way below the road level and some more road bends till you see the Baptist Theological Seminary up on the hill to the left. From there, after a few more sharp bends, it is only 2km (1¼ miles) to the hotel belt of **Batu Ferringhi**. Along the way, you will see an army camp on the right, followed immediately afterwards by the **Rasa Sayang Resort**.

Batu Ferringhi, or Portuguese Rock, is named after the first Europeans who landed here in Penang during the early 15th century. It is now dominated by a stretch of highrise hotels, shops and restaurants. Watersports is a perennial attraction along the shoreline. Its golden strip is where bodies are bared to worship the monocled eye of the sun, albeit with a generous slathering of sun block lotion.

The Rasa Sayang, Palm Beach and Golden Sands resorts stand in a row to the right of the seafront. They all belong to the Shangri-La International chain of hotels. Lone Pine Hotel, Holiday Inn, Parkroyal, Casuarina Beach Hotel and Bayview Beach are also sea-facing properties just up the road. The hotel properties, with their sprawling compounds, are 50m (54½yds) from the high tide shore-

Mutiara Beach Resort

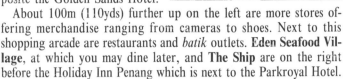

line, to ensure no obstruction of the sandy beach.

Along this stretch of Batu Ferringhi are seafood restaurants such as **Adam's Terrace**, **Eve's Gardenia** and **Fisherman's Wharf**. The Sriwani Tax Free Emporium is on the left opposite the Golden Sands Hotel.

About 100m (110yds) further up on the left are more stores offering merchandise ranging from cameras to shoes. Next to this shopping arcade are restaurants and *batik* outlets. **Eden Seafood Village**, at which you may dine later, and **The Ship** are on the right before the Holiday Inn Penang which is next to the Parkroyal Hotel.

Some 50m (54½yds) down to the left from here are the Batu Ferringhi police station and post office. Also on the same side of the road are **Yahong Art Gallery** and **Penang Village Restaurant**. **Papa Din Bamboo** and **Happy Garden** are two local eating houses about 200m (220yds) up the road before the Casuarina Beach Hotel looms up to the right. Next to this is the highrise Bayview Beach Resort.

Another 10km (6¼ miles) straight up the winding but scenic coastal road is **Teluk Bahang** which means 'the bay of reflected

light', for at noon, the sea here shimmers scintillatingly. The luxurious **Penang Mutiara Beach Resort** is sited near the village centre comprising some coffeeshops and stores, as is the market, which is 200m (220yds) down the road after the roundabout. Villagers go there to buy fish, meat and vegetables for their daily meals. A regular morning activity is the gathering of vendors selling food, clothing and household wares on the roadside near the roundabout.

About 500m (545yds) up the road is **Kampung Nelayan**, which means 'fishermen's village'. The fishing community resides at the end of the beach after the market near a wooden pier, where all the sea-going vessels anchor offshore in the bay. About 400 families live in small houses in the neighbourhood. Where the road terminates is the restaurant known facetiously as **'The End of the World'**. Run by proprietor Ah Sim who serves fresh seafood, it is usually crowded. Advance reservations are advised. Orders for lobster thermidor, tiger prawns, chilli crabs and steamed pomfret must be placed early for the sup-

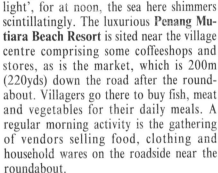

Kampung Nelayan

plies are limited. As a landmark, it is the starting point for trekkers going to Muka Head, Pantai Aceh and Pantai Kerachut.

Craft Batik, 100m (110yds) from the village roundabout, is a factory producing ready-to-wear and printed *batik*. The staff will give guided tours of the busy workshop and explain the various stages of using wax and dye to create complicated designs inspired by floral patterns and shapes.

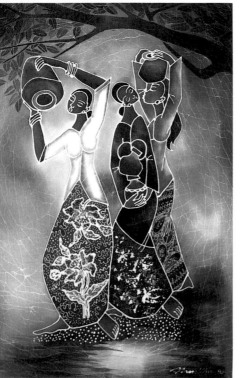

Vibrant designs at Craft Batik

Garments, fabrics and handicrafts are displayed for sale in the showroom, which opens from 9am to 5pm daily.

The **Penang Butterfly Farm** about 2km (1¼ miles) away from Craft Batik is a repository of gentle, fragile-winged beauties. Considered the largest of its kind ever since its opening in 1986, it has over 4,000 tropical butterflies of some 120 species that roam freely in a natural environment full of greenery and flora. Uncaged birds in the huge enclosure are seed-feeders and live harmoniously with the butterflies.

Live black scorpions are found in a wire net-covered pit where visitors can study them from a safe distance. Unusual live exhibits include the moving leaf and stick insects.

Rare jungle creatures like the tree climbing frog, dead leaf toad, giant millipede, chameleons, water-dragons, spiders and other unique specimens from the living equatorial forest are kept in glass tanks and cages. Inside this educational park, which is a breeding and research centre for butterflies, are three garden ponds containing fishes, terrapins and swimming ducks.

The Insect Museum shows the colour and beauty of the insect kingdom. Some 2,000 specimens comprising 600 species of butterflies and moths and 800 species of beetles and other insects are displayed.

Open throughout the year, visiting hours are 9am to 5pm on weekdays and till 6pm on weekends and public holidays. The entry fee is RM4 per adult and RM2 for children under 12 years. A surcharge of RM1 is collected for cameras and RM3 for video cameras. There is a large, free parking lot outside. Refreshments are sold in the gift shop which sells framed insects, butterfly souvenirs, T-shirts, kites, toys, jewellery and curios.

It should be dusk by the time you finish at the butterfly farm.

Green, peace and fragile beauty at the Butterfly Farm

Adjourn to the **Pinang Cultural Centre** (Tel: 812-828) next to
Mutiara Beach Resort in Teluk Bahang for a meal and enjoy the
45-minute Malaysian folk dance show held daily. Showtime is at
10.45am, 1, 3.30, 8.30 and 10.30pm. Admission fee is RM17 per
adult, RM7 per child aged 8-12 years and free to those younger.
An exhibition area displays local heritage artifacts and costumes,
and a bazaar sells handicrafts. Or else, return to Batu Ferringhi
and dine at the **Eden Seafood Village** where you are entertained by
a live band and a local variety spectacle that begins at 8.30pm.

PICK & MIX

These half-day excursions offer a selection of short and interesting tour options which can be combined in any way you wish to suit your schedule. Each tour provides an insight into typical Penang lifestyles and scenes.

Morning Itineraries

1. Breakfasts and Morning Markets

An early start for breakfast and browsing at Penang's wet and dry markets.

An early morning meal with the residents is one good way to sample a slice of local life. Sunrise is around 6.30am and though the city is generally still asleep, some key locations are alive with activity. However, remember that Sundays and holidays are slack times for people-watching, with the residents taking a well-deserved siesta.

Penang's wet and dry markets are marvellous spots to wander about for the early riser. You get to see the people vociferously buying and selling produce like vegetables, fruits, meat, fish and other foodstuffs. You also have the chance to try local cuisine at the foodstalls.

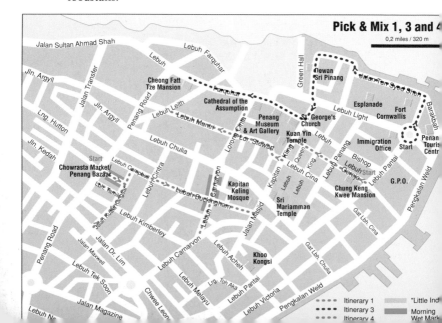

Bustling Jalan Kuala Kangsar market

Take a taxi to George Town and tell the driver to drop you at the **Chowrasta** market (also mentioned in *Day 1*). Provision shops line the front of the market at Penang Road. Inside, it is dark and slippery. On the upper level is an indoor bazaar with stalls selling clothes and souvenirs.

Go to the back streets which are packed with food sellers and housewives. **Jalan Kuala Kangsar** right behind the Chowrasta market is barely passable to vehicular traffic. Occasionally, a bicycle or motorbike may slip through but with much difficulty as the place is packed like a can of sardines with people and stalls.

If you care to see more, walk down **Jalan Kuala Kangsar** and turn right to Lebuh Campbell whose shops open for business after 9am. Go for another 250m (272½yds) on this street till you arrive at the **Lebuh Carnarvon** T-junction. Right here is another wet market within a building with an antiquated arch tower façade. In the neighbouring streets, espe-

Succulent sea cucumbers

cially on **Lebuh Buckingham**, many hawkers ply their trade.

One km (½ miles) away down to the end of Lebuh Carnarvon on your left near the KOMTAR Complex is the wholesale market at **Jalan Prangin**. If you are keen to see it come alive,

get out at sunrise, for this market already starts to bustle hours before dawn. Lorries and trucks bring fresh produce in the wee hours of the morning. Vegetables and fruits are sold by the basketful though you can always buy the individual piece if you wish. This is the place to buy salted fish and other dried foodstuffs such as black mushrooms, red dates, *gingko* nuts and other edibles.

If you like markets, the one at **Pulau Tikus** in **Jalan Pasar** deserves a look. Go there by cab in the morning. This market has the reputation for selling the most expensive but freshest produce. Many refer to it as the rich man's market. Most locals go there to buy its takeaway *nonya* cooked foods which are sold in the tiny, crowded lane to the right of the market building. Inside, to the left behind the cloth merchants, are more stalls selling cakes, noodles and soya bean milk.

At **Fettes Park** in **Tanjung Tokong**, goods are sold cheaply at the **Tanjung Bungah** market opposite the police station. Many more vendors spread their fruits, vegetables and flowers on the roadside.

The markets are easy to locate if you are coming down from the beach hotel area in Batu Ferringhi. Most taxi drivers know where they are. For a mini-version of a local Penang market, visit the spot across the road from the Golden Sands Hotel. Each morning, mobile vans and vendors make a stop to cater to the needs of housewives living in the area.

If you are more adventurous and wish to explore a larger place, the **Air Itam** market is big and attracts many shoppers in search of bargains. The fresh produce comes from the hill slopes where vegetables, fruits and flowers are cultivated. Meat and seafood are sold inside while a tempting selection of cooked food can be found outside the market building.

To get a feel of what the rustic Penang island farms produce, you should visit the quaint town of **Balik Pulau**, which has a large market established since 1914. The market is on the main road in the town centre. During the local fruit season, city folk venture there to purchase durians, rambutans, pineapples, mangoes and melons. Balik Pulau is rather far from the city as it is on the

other side of the island from George Town, but the trip is pleasant and scenic. Most taxi drivers know the way.

2. On the Waterfront

The godowns at Pengkalan Weld; Swettenham Pier to see the ships; breakfast with office workers; explore the water village in Weld Quay; lunch at a local eating stall.

Pengkalan Weld (Weld Quay), which runs along the harbour, has a row of godowns dating from the turn of the 20th century. Built by major European trading agencies to store goods along the quay facing the harbour, these have been converted into office buildings. Some still exist in their original structures though several have been

Penang Port

Ride a trishaw

modified, fitted with airconditioning and repainted, their facades featuring multiple arches and columns.

Seek out this stretch of edifices behind the **General Post Office** in **Lebuh Downing** which has a corridor clogged with parked bicycles and motorcycles. The sidewalk stalls and coffeeshops here rely on the patronage of port labourers and office workers. Take note: activities on Sundays and holidays are scarce.

Right next to the main office building in Lebuh Downing is the telecoms office where you can make overseas telephone calls and send telegrams and telexes (open 24 hours a day). Have a snack in the side lane next to the Hongkong and Shanghai Bank where the local *teh tarik* (literally, pulled tea), piping hot tea with milk is served with a flourish and stalls sell rice and noodles for breakfast and lunch.

Another good place to eat is directly opposite the Hongkong and Shanghai Bank. This is the **Kedai Makanan Yong Sing** next to the Barkath Store on Lebuh Union, which is beside the Standard Chartered Bank. Here, you can find *nasi kandar*, noodles and freshly-made banana pancakes with raisins and sesame seeds, among other goodies.

Penang Port Commission Building

The principal wharves of George Town's harbour are at **Swettenham Pier**. This is behind the **Penang Port Commission** (PPC) building which in turn is across the big carpark in front of the post office. It is where cruise liners and cargo ships berth. Permission for entry is only granted to boat passengers, cargo agents and port workers.

Ekspres Perdana, the air-conditioned, high-speed luxury ferry service to Pulau Langkawi and Belawan port in Sumatra, can be

Chinese temple on stilts

boarded from here. The 200-seat ferry has modern facilities which include a cafeteria, souvenir shop, TV, video and karaoke entertainment. The ferry goes to **Pulau Langkawi** daily and to **Belawan** on Monday, Wednesday, Friday and Saturday. The ticket office, Kuala Perlis–Langkawi Ferry Service Sdn Bhd (Tel: 625-630, 625-631), is next to the Penang Tourist Centre in the shopping arcade of the PPC office block. Ekspres Bahagia (Langkawi) Sdn Bhd (Tel: 631-943, 635-255) immediately next door also has four sailings to Belawan per week. Free transportation is provided from Belawan port to Medan town in Sumatra, Indonesia.

About 800m (870yds) to the left of the PPC on Pengkalan Weld is the **Weld Quay A North pier** which serves crew arriving and returning to ships in the harbour roads. Another 400m (436yds) to its left is the bus depot at Pengkalan Weld, just beside the ferry terminus and caters to those going to or coming from Butterworth. Four bus services start and end here. They are Sri Negara, Lim Seng Seng, Penang Yellow Bus and Hin Bus companies. These run to the north, south and centre of the island.

The non-stop ferry boat service which runs regularly between George Town and Butterworth can be boarded at about 100m (110yds) to the right at **Pengkalan Raja Tun Uda**. Double-decker ferries carry passengers on the top deck and vehicles below. Several ferries transport only cars, buses, vans, lorries and motorcycles.

Adjacent to the ferry terminus to the right is a cluster of homes on stilts. A series of plank bridges connect houses standing in the sea. Many families belonging to different clans reside in this water village. The menfolk are harbour workers such as stevedores and chandlers. Many load and unload cargo for a living from the ships that call in the port. They carry the goods in lighter boats that chug out to the anchored vessels and back to the shore again. Stroll along the wooden walkways and catch a glimpse of life in this settlement that began in the late 19th century. A small Chinese temple is found on the shore in front of the village.

For lunch, if you are willing to wait, go to **Eam Huat** (Tel: 621-751), situated on the lane beside the covered hawker centre about 400m (436yds) opposite the ferry terminus in Lebuh Victoria. This coffee shop gets very packed during lunch hour and its regular customers queue for the famous beef soup which costs RM3 to RM5 for small to large servings eaten with steamed rice or flat rice noodles (*koay teow*). It opens from 9am till 6.30pm.

Alternatively, you can seek out the coffee shops at **Lebuh Gereja** (as Church Street is now called) which have shrimp fritters and other delights. They are behind the Kee Huat Radio shop on Lebuh Pantai and near the Phoenix Press in Lebuh Gereja.

Return to the ferry terminus to get a cab at the taxi stand or catch a bus from the depot next to it.

3. Historical Quarter

Walk around Fort Cornwallis, once used to defend the island; visit the Penang Museum and Art Gallery; lunch and then to the 19th-century Cheong Fatt Tze mansion.

History buffs will enjoy the relics and monuments from Penang's rich past, which still stand very well preserved today. Outstanding examples of colonial architecture that exist in this oldest part of George Town can be discovered by taking a walking tour.

Tell the taxi driver to take you to the **Immigration** office at Lebuh Pantai in George Town. The Moorish-style clock tower

Francis Light Statue at Penang Museum

stands opposite the office, behind a roundabout decorated with giant metal hibiscus blooms, the Malaysian national flower. Next to the clock tower on the right is the **Penang Tourist Centre**, located in the Penang Port Commission Building shopping arcade. The northern region office of the **Malaysia Tourism Promotion Board** is about 50m (54½yds) round the corner towards the fort. Both places provide information on Penang.

The white clock tower built in 1897 stands at 18.2m (60ft) high and was meant to commemorate the diamond jubilee of Queen Victoria's reign – each foot of the tower denotes a year

Right, the dignified clock tower

State Legislative Building

of her rule over *Pax Britannica*. It was donated to George Town by a local wealthy Chinese businessman.

The large and hard to avoid **Fort Cornwallis**, on Jalan Tun Syed Sheh Barakbah next to the clock tower, replaced a wooden stockade originally put up by the founder of Penang, Captain Francis Light. The brick and mortar walls were constructed by convicts from 1808 to 1810 to defend the island, and the fort once had a moat which was filled in during the 1920s.

Approach the entrance to Fort Cornwallis from the waterfront side. The brick walls have ramparts still fitted with cannons. Climb up to the big mounted cannon known locally as Seri Rambai, originally from Holland and manufactured in 1618. Inside the fort complex is an old chapel, former prison cells and a park. An amphitheatre in the open grounds of the fort is often used for cultural shows.

At the northeast corner of the fort is a lighthouse that looks like a ship's mast. Not accessible to the public, it is nonetheless an interesting sight as it looks like an old clipper ship minus the bow and body. The lighthouse overlooks **Kedah pier** where the **Penang Yacht Club** is sited. It offers berthing facilities for leisure sailing craft in its marina.

Behind the fort, on Lebuh Light and facing the **Esplanade** is the **State Legislative Building**. It is a collonaded building with the words 'Dewan Undangan Negeri' on its facade. Next door to this is the Mariner's Club. Directly opposite is Medan Selera, a covered hawker centre beside the fort which is next to the roller skating rink.

The town green or the Esplanade, also called Padang

At the Esplanade

Kota Lama, is an open field for public events and football games. Once jungle shrouded, Captain Light ordered his soldiers to trim the dense vegetation in search of the Spanish silver dollar coins that he had placed into a cannon and fired into the trees. It was here that the British landed and the Union Jack was first hoisted in 1786.

One of the two Anglo-style buildings dating from 1903, at the far end of the Esplanade opposite the fort, houses College Damansara Utama, a private college for pre-university preparatory studies. The other bigger edifice nearer the sea is the Municipal City Hall built in 1897. To their left on the seawall front is a cenotaph which commemorates those who died in the war.

Jalan Tun Syed Sheh Barakbah, which starts behind the clock tower and ends beside the Dewan Sri Pinang, is one busy food street. By late afternoon, many foodstalls are open for business in the permanent hawker centre and on the walkway behind the old City Hall building. It becomes really active after sundown and at night when many people flock here for a late supper.

Dewan Sri Pinang, a multi-purpose hall for exhibitions and concerts has its main entrance on Lebuh Light opposite the Bank Negara (National Bank). A large theatre inside can accommodate up to 3,000 people. The public Penang Library (Tel: 622-255) which is open to the public, is located on the second floor.

For lunch, try *Peranakan* cuisine at **Dragon King**, 99 Lebuh Bishop just behind the Bank Negara. Here, you get authentic Straits Chinese dishes. The air-conditioned restaurant is usually

Cathedral of the Assumption

Cheong Fatt Tze Mansion, excellent turn-of-the-century Chinese architecture

packed – proof of how good the food is. Try and get there before 12 noon to ensure a table. Takeaways are also done. The restaurant represents Penang home-style cooking at its commercial best.

After lunch, head towards the left to where St George's Church stands at the beginning of Lebuh Farquhar behind Bank Negara. Right next to this Anglican landmark is the **Penang Museum & Art Gallery** whose building dates from 1817. A treasure house of material culture and historic relics, it is open daily from 9am to 5pm, but closed from 12.15 to 2.45pm on Fridays. No photography is permitted and admission is free. A life-sized bronze statue of Captain Light stands outside the building under frangipani trees blooming with white flowers.

The **High Court** building which faces the museum has large grounds and a stone memorial dedicated to James R Logan, a British lawyer, editor and public servant who died in 1869. Directly opposite is another historic place, the **Convent Light Street**, a girl's school founded by Carmelite sisters from France.

To the right, 50m (54½yds) along Lebuh Farquhar, is the **Cathedral of the Assumption** for Roman Catholics. To its immediate left is St Xavier's Institution, a boy's school started in 1852 by the La Sallian Christian brothers.

Behind the school, about 300m (330yds) away to the left in Lebuh Leith, is the **Cheong Fatt Tze mansion**, which has cobblestone courtyards, gables, moon windows and red roof tiles. Facing this splendid mansion is a fine arts conservatory. Many people consider the Cheong Fatt Tze mansion one of the finest examples of classical 19th-century Chinese architecture existing outside China. Its original household antiques have been auctioned off, but the large rooms and hallways have rich interiors, a steel spiral stairway and carved wall partitions. Restored to its former glory, it is worth a visit for a feel of old Cathay transported to Southeast Asian shores.

Right, lighthouse at Fort Cornwallis

Lorong Stewart

Afternoon Itineraries

4. Ethnic Discoveries

A leisurely walk around Chinatown, Little India, the suburbs, or Pulau Tikus. Get to know more about George Town's ethnic enclaves and Penang's 'Thailand'. These passages are descriptive. They are suggested itineraries and not meant to be done in sequence. Read through, choose those places you wish to see and plan your routes according to your schedule. A helpful hint: should you want to do Chinatown and Little India together, start from Lebuh Muntri back to Lebuh Gereja.

Chinatown: A stroll through the streets gives an insight into the lifestyles of those who came from China in the 1800s as George Town prospered. Parallel rows of shophouses reflect the heritage left behind to their descendants. Their backstreets are narrow, originally built as passages for rickshaws and carts, and are therefore inaccessible to vehicles.

Chinatown sprawls from the **harbour** to **Lorong Stewart, Lebuh Muntri** and **Lebuh Campbell**. This is one of the largest and best-preserved overseas Chinese enclaves in Southeast Asia.

You might like to take a trip into the city's rich past by visiting the **Chung Keng Kwee** ancestral hall and temple complex at No. 29 Lebuh Gereja, formerly the headquarters of illegal secret societies. Take a taxi from your hotel to Lebuh Gereja.

The temple complex comprises an ancient wall, small lanes and walled courtyards. Formerly the home of Chung Keng Kwee, who became the Chinese community leader in George Town in 1893, it has since been given a European look. The gate was fitted with a cast iron grille and bay windows were installed. A private temple in Kwangtung style was erected next door. Today, the statue of Chung Keng Kwee garbed in Mandarin robes graces the ancestral hall.

Home of Chung Keng Kwee holds long-ago secret society intrigues

Street puppet theatre

Though still closed to the public, the mansion is worth viewing from the outside; its façade behind the iron fence and gate is a unique blend of western and eastern decorative artwork and architecture. From the mansion, make your way down Lebuh Gereja for about 500m (545yds) and then turn left into **Lebuh Klng**. On the right side of the street is the **Nin Yong Temple** and a row of Chinese clan houses with dark interiors. Ask permission to take pictures.

Exit to the right into Lebuh China. About 400m (436yds) down and across the street is the **Kuan Yin Teng Temple** in Jalan Masjid Kapitan Keling (as mentioned in *Day 2*). Immediately behind it is **Lorong Stewart**. Make your way slowly along this narrow lane with houses on both sides. It ends in **Lorong Cinta** (Love Lane), which is wider and easier to walk along without feeling squeezed or hemmed in.

Straight on from Lorong Stewart after the T-junction with Lorong Cinta is **Lebuh Muntri**, where you will find solid double storey houses with 'five-foot ways' (pavements) forming long corridors in front of home entrances ending at **Lebuh Leith** after about 1km (½ mile). Opposite the X-junction of Lebuh Muntri and Lebuh Leith stands the small **Kedai Kopi Lum Fong** coffeeshop. A booking desk outside accepts bookings for taxi rides to Hatyai in South Thailand, in case you wish to take a side trip across the border. The five-hour overland journey costs about M$20 per person one-way.

If you continue for another 20m (22yds) you will come to Penang Road, where you can get some refreshments before hailing a cab back to your hotel.

Little India: Under British colonial rule, many Indian migrants were brought to Penang during the 19th century to work in the plantations and on the

Behind the scenes

Indian Muslim Mosque

railroads. These Indian pioneers came with their unique culture and sank new roots in the British-controlled port towns along the Straits of Malacca.

Till today, settlers of Indian origin in George Town are largely found in **Lebuh Pantai** and **Jalan Masjid Kapitan Keling**, which are the financial streets where banks and money changers thrive. The area flanked by these two streets has a distinctly Indian character, earning it the name 'Little India'.

Lebuh Pantai was previously known by its anglicised name, Beach Street; thus called because the sea used to lap against its shore a long time ago. The name 'Beach Street' lives on despite the tides having receded since the turn of the century. Today, many buildings have been erected along the former shoreline.

Jalan Masjid Kapitan Keling has many Indian jewellery stores and licensed money changers who will accept foreign currencies at better rates than at banks. The Indians and Indian-Muslims who dominate the money changing trade reside mainly in the neighbourhood of Lebuh Penang, Lebuh King and Lebuh Queen. The three streets are parallel to and within walking distance of each other. To get to this area, walk about 200m (220yds) straight down from Lebuh Pantai at its junction with **Lebuh Pasar** (Market Street) where the Overseas Union Bank, and the SMN Shaik Mohamed money changer and general merchant store stand on the left and right respectively.

Lebuh Pasar is lined with shops run by Indians. The grocery shops sell a variety of spices and other goods. Checked *pulicat sarongs*, cotton materials and fabrics are displayed

Indian cake vendor to hail when hungry

Lebuh Pantai (Beach Street)

cheek by jowl with bangles, earrings and costume jewellery. **Syarikat Ilahi Trading** at No. 31 Lebuh Pasar is a wholesaler in spices, grains, pulses and other goods imported from India. **Sree Meenambigai Store** at No. 37 sells ethnic clothing, silverware and brassware.

The Chettiar community, which specialises in private money-lending, conducts its business in Little India. You may spy Chettiar members sitting cross-legged in the halls of the shophouses as you stroll by. Each has a chest which serves as a desk. Prospective borrowers sit on a low stool to negotiate a credit transaction, all very discreet and above board.

Sundry shops in the vicinity of both Lebuh Penang and Lebuh Queen have the pungent scent of spices, the fragrance of incense and the gleam of metallic ware. They lead into **Lebuh Chulia** (named after the Chulia Indian community), a street where many Indian textile merchants specialise in Benares silk and *saree* fabrics.

Sometimes, you may see sliced betelnut (*pinang*) sun dried in the streets before being packed and exported to India where the practice of betel quid chewing still prevails.

Located at No. 41 Lebuh Penang is Darshan Acupuncture and Ayurvedic Centre, right next door to the popular **Kaliamans Restaurant** which specialises in North Indian cuisine. **Veloo Villas** at No. 22 Lebuh Penang is a simple restaurant serving *thosai* (rice flour pancakes), curries and vegetarian food. Or else, seek out **Dawood Restaurant** at No. 63 Lebuh Queen which serves delicious curries. It faces the main entrance of the Sri Maha Mariamman temple. Try the tasty chicken or mutton *masala*, and *lassi*, a mild and refreshing yogurt drink to go with the hot food.

Suburbia: If you want to get a feel of how Penang's middle class and very wealthy live, or if you simply have a penchant for town planning and architecture, spend some time scouring Penang's prime residential districts. The best way to do this tour is to hire a self-drive car or charter a taxi for the day. The districts mentioned

are in close vicinity to each other. If you choose to drive, equip yourself with a good Penang street map.

Penang's middle class reside outside George Town in new satellite townships. Such places have sprung up only since the 1960s to alleviate the shortage of housing in the city districts.

Green Lane is now known as **Jalan Masjid Negeri**. There are many rows of terrace houses in the area after the Penang Free School and the Convent Green Lane. The main residential estates are Green Garden, Island Park, Island Glades and Taman Ghee Hiang. Most of the houses are new concrete buildings with tiled roofs. Many are single or double-storey constructions with small plots of gardens in front and a parking lot under the porch.

Taman Brown, Minden and **Bandar Bayan Baru** are about 15 minutes away by car out of the city. Buses and taxis go to these suburban outskirt districts regularly throughout the day.

The bourgeoisie have their luxurious homes on **Jalan Cantonment**, **Jalan Brown** and **Jalan Jesselton** within the general Pulau Tikus area. Towards George Town, a number of grand, Anglo-style mansions along royal palm-lined **Lebuhraya Peel** add charm and character to the city. Most were built in the 1920s and 1930s and are worth a scrutiny.

The homes along **Jalan Sultan Ahmad Shah** near the roundabout with **Pesiaran Gurney** and **Jalan Pangkor** are outstanding. Some are palatial houses with manicured lawns in big gardens at the end of long driveways. Their frontage is pillared and have broad

Scenes from suburbia

porches, wide steps and airy verandahs. Wealthy families have resided in them for generations. These domains of the rich were constructed by British-trained architects during the rubber and tin boom years before the Great Depression and World War II.

Around Pulau Tikus: On foot, you will see a bit of 'Thailand' in Penang, catch a glimpse of Burma, saunter through Jalan Cantonment to the Youth Park and have an early dinner at a nearby restaurant.

The name **Pulau Tikus** translates as 'Rat Isle' and refers to a tiny, uninhabited place with a light beacon located offshore in **Tanjung Bungah**. But many people use it to refer to a general area from **Jalan Jones** and **Lebuhraya Codrington** onwards to the end of **Jalan Burma** near the Seventh Day Adventist Hospital about 4km (2½ miles) from Jalan Penang. This route is for steadfast walkers as you would have to walk nearly 3km (1¾ miles). It is a pleasant walk under shady trees, otherwise hire a cab.

Locals seek out its market at **Jalan Pasar** for *nyonya* cakes and cooked food which are sold along the pavement every morning. The coffeeshops behind the market at **Solok Moulmein** are popular haunts for breakfast, lunch and dinner. A bus stop directly across offers easy access to the coffeeshops.

Just behind the market is **Lorong Burmah**, the location of two major Theravada Buddhist temples sought by pilgrims and tourists alike. Each faces the other and their entrances draw visitors continually. Peddlers sell everything from T-shirts printed with the Penang map, cheap sunglasses and slippers to fruits and drinks on the sidewalks.

Wat Chaiya Mangkalaram, founded in 1845, is a gaudy but intriguing temple. Guardian dragons and tall statues greet you outside the building. They are painted in lurid colours of red,

Wat Chaiya Mangkalaram

Dharmmikarama Burmese Temple

green, turquoise, orange, white and ochre. Inside is a 33-m (108-ft) long figure of the reclining Buddha covered in gold leaf. Below and behind is a columbarium where ashes of Buddhists are kept in urns. Wall frescoes and panel reliefs depict the life history of Prince Siddharta, who attained enlightenment as Gautama Buddha.

Admission is free, but shoes must be left outside. A sign warns: 'Beware of shoe thieves!'. So be wise and place your footwear in a plastic bag and carry them with you as you tour the temple. The same signboard also warns: 'Photography is forbidden'. To get around this no-picture-taking policy of the gilt-covered interiors, snap your photos at the doorstep.

A graveyard lies behind and several other buildings are in the wide temple grounds. Limited parking space is available in front of the four-faced Buddha statue under the trees.

The **Dharmmikarama Burmese Temple**, the second temple on this road, has an arched doorway with sculptured elephants. Its two authentic Burmese *stupas* are dazzlingly lit at night, especially on the first and fifteenth days of the Chinese lunar calendar. Originally founded in 1803, it is the largest Theravada Buddhist temple in Penang. The landscaped gardens have an intricate Burmese style pagoda with layered roofs built above a pond and a profoundly philosphical sign, 'Big fish eat small ones', advising against letting fish into it. Many visitors like to throw coins onto a square board floating on the water as you are bestowed with good luck if you succeed in doing so.

If you visit during the **Water Festival** each April, be prepared to be doused. Adults join the young to throw buckets of water at one another. This traditional act of purification has been modified by using rubber hoses. When caught in such a situation, many smile and return the compliment by drenching the other party.

After temple viewing in Lorong Burmah, turn left and walk 200m (220yds) to **Jalan Burmah**. Go down the road to the traffic lights junction with **Jalan Cantonment**. Exit left and stroll about 1km (½ mile) till you reach **Jalan Macalister**. Along the way are large bungalows with sprawling gardens. It is quite a pleasant walk as the route is shaded by tall, old trees which have a broad canopy of leaves that keep the temperature down and effectively screen the glare of the sun.

Turn right into Jalan Macalister and walk 450m (490½yds) to the end where the traffic lights are. At this junction, turn right again and you will find yourself on **Jalan Utama**. About 500m (545yds) straight on the left is the **Youth Park** or **Taman Belia Perbandaran** in Quarry Drive which is accessible across a short bridge from Jalan Utama, just off the end of Jalan Macalister. It has a large parking lot and numerous amusement facilities, including swings and rope obstacle courses and a playground for children. A small, rippling brook flowing through it makes the park an ideal setting for picnics. Just beware of monkeys foraging for food.

After you have toured the Youth Park, retrace your steps to Jalan Utama for another kilometre. At its end, before the road leading to the Botanical Gardens, is **Jalan Gottlieb**, which has some ideal dining spots. Try the **Hotel Waterfall** (Tel: 370-887) which has western set meals and an a la carte menu. Close by is **Dragon Inn** (Tel: 379-049), a small family-style restaurant that serves good meals. The bigger double-storey **Prosperous Restaurant** (Tel: 361-736) caters to tour groups, wedding banquets and private parties. You can arrange with the restaurant staff for a taxi back to your hotel afterwards.

5. Nature Walks

A ramble through lush greenery at two different nature parks. Choose between the verdant Botanical Gardens or the Forest Recreation Park.

Botanical Gardens: Also known as Taman Kebun Bunga, the more than a century old gardens is sited in 30ha (74 acres) of valley land. Popularly called 'Waterfall' because of a cascade in its hills, it was begun by the British in 1884. The gardens close after 7pm daily. To get there, catch the MPPP bus No. 7 from the Pengkalan Weld bus terminal (30 minutes from here) or the bus station in KOMTAR (a 20-minute journey).

If you choose to drive, follow the signboard placed at the Bagan Jermal roundabout near Sunrise Tower. Go on Jalan Gottlieb which is lined with royal palms until the end of the road, then turn right into **Jalan Air Terjun** (Waterfall Road) and drive into the parking area outside the gardens. No vehicles are allowed within the garden grounds except those belonging to the staff. The gardens are strictly for pedestrians. No skateboards, roller-skates and bicycles are permitted either.

The gardens, open from 7am–7pm, are visited at all times of the day. In the mornings, joggers are a common sight. You may also watch a group of people performing *tai-chi* exercises, which resemble *kung fu* fighting in much slower motion. Later in the morning, tourists come by to view the lush vegetation. As evening approaches, many people come for leisurely strolls, enjoying the fresh air. The ringing sound carried by the breeze is likely to be cicadas rubbing their wings together in the trees.

A public park with trees and shrubs, greenhouses and well-planted groves, the Botanical Gardens is home to the pig-tailed monkeys or macaques. Pesky vendors tout peanuts to feed the bands

Botanical Gardens and the replica of Penang Bridge

of furry creatures. Try offering them fruits such as bananas, but be careful as they can be rather bold – they normally make the first move as soon as they spot a human visitor with food. The tamer ones will take goodies from your hands, but the bolder monkeys snatch whole bags of peanuts which they stuff into their mouths. Some monkeys may also fancy iced drinks and sweets.

Two loop roads are used by joggers and walkers. The lower circle route goes around the stream where children can catch tadpoles and tiny fishes in the clear waters. Families often picnic beside it. A bandstand is found in the centre of the park near the bridgeway modelled after the big Penang Bridge. This road is relatively flat all the way.

Large clumps of bamboo, ferns and palms are interspersed with ironwood, banyan and raintrees throughout the park. All are tagged with common and Latin names. There is a small corner with different types of lawn grasses. From this spot, you can glimpse the waterfall far in the distance. It looks like a metallic strip glinting in the sunshine amidst the green-shrouded jungle.

The 100-m (110-yd) path to the **water lily pond** is dark and cool. It is found near the mini-zoo along the lower circular road. At the entrance is a tall tree with huge, gnarled buttress roots that extend 2m (6½ft) from its trunk. This *petai jawa* or *parkia javanica* has bitter seeds that are of local medicinal value. Park benches are found in shady corners near the lily pond. Rub some citronella oil on your ears, neck and hands to ward off mosquitoes. A signboard warns of a RM500 fine if you let a tortoise loose into the pond. The reason is because many Buddhists release tiny tortoises bought from pet shops into the lily pond to gain merit, and these creatures feast on the water lilies.

The upper loop road goes by a reservoir that is out of bounds. A notice board states menacingly: 'Trespassers will be prosecuted' and shows a gun pointed at a figure as illustration to convey the message. Running up this steep route is more challenging than the flat stretch below. On the way down, stop by the Malayan honey bear pit and sambar deer enclosure. The route connects back to the lower circle. A big **orchidarium** has opened nearby. The 0.1-ha (¼-acre) complex is sited on a steep gradient which is landscaped with a waterfall. Its live orchid collection comprises many fine examples of the reputed 800 species that exist in both Peninsular and East Malaysia.

A more arduous climb is the hour-long trek up to the big waterfall which plunges 92m (300ft) down in the hills. Walk up to the filtration plant in the Botanical Gardens to reach the path that leads there. Permission is needed though the permit is easy to get from the **Pihak Berkuasa Air (Penang Water Authority)** at the City Council office, KOMTAR, level three (Tel: 625-321). This waterfall attraction is only open to the public on weekends and public holidays from 2pm to 6pm.

Forest Recreation Park and Forestry Museum: The 100-ha (247-acre) ecotourist attraction, also known as **Rimba Rekreasi** in Teluk Bahang is in an arboretum with a running stream and pond. There is ample parking space for cars and coaches.

You have to go northeast to explore the beauty of this equatorial rainforest. To reach it, turn left at the village roundabout at Teluk Bahang. Go straight for about 800m (872yds) past the mosque, hospital, school, Green Orchid nursery and the Butterfly Farm. The park is on the left side of the road. It is located about 50m (54½yds) before the butterfly farm and less than 1km (½ mile) after the *batik* factory.

The huge parkland has facilities for picnickers. Highlights include a fish pond, wading pool, children's playground and plant nursery. Many indigenous tree species along with exotic botanical specimens are to be found there. Huge signs with maps and directions to these attractions are found in the park. Benches for your picnic lunch or tea are found under shady trees.

As you enter the park, you will see the **Forestry Museum** which has exhibits of flora and natural vegetation aimed at informing visitors about the equatorial rainforest, its products and uses. Basic information about forestry subjects represented by dioramas and special sections devoted to silviculture, ethnobotany, entomology, jungle produce and wood processing are displayed.

Move on further behind the museum to find several walking trails that lead into the jungle. Shelter huts, a playground and canteen are located at this lush green, outdoor recreational centre. Its environs offer an insight into the ancient 130 million-year-old Malaysian rainforest. For easy identification, the trees are tagged with their local common and Latin botanical names.

The visiting hours for the recreation park are from 7am to 7pm daily. The Forestry Museum (Tel: 811-280) is open from 9am to 5pm everyday except Monday. Admission fee is 50 sen per adult and 30 sen per child. Car parking is free.

Right, cocoa pods and the ubiquitous durian

Nightlife

Night Markets

Check out the nocturnal markets for local colour and a spot of haggling and shopping.

The *pasar malam*, or night market, is the venue for the evening shopping ritual before and after dinner. Families often embark on this outing with gusto. All kinds of delicious food and consumer items are available at these make-shift bazaars.

Never mind if you haven't had dinner yet, part of the lure is the chance to indulge in tidbits and light snacks. Mobile stalls peddle steamed peanuts, corn-on-the-cob, sliced fruit, drinks and cakes. As you pick your way through the night market, you will come across fake designer T-shirts, cassette tapes and household necessities such as mothballs, kitchenware and plastic goods. The variety is staggering, the choice enticing and the prices quite painless. The scene is mainly for locals but visitors will enjoy the easy-going atmosphere and the stalls laden with bric-a-brac.

The hawkers move to different designated venues once every two weeks, opening for business from 7pm till 11pm at each site. There are five main sites for the mobile market.

Check with your hotel reception on where to go on the day you are keen to experience *pasar malam*. As it is a nomadic market, you must know its exact location before making your trip. For additional information, please check with the **City Health Department**, which is in charge of the night markets (Tel: 624-400). The best time to call is around 2pm.

Some tips: you get what you pay for, so forget about after sales service for the 'Rolex' or 'Cartier' wristwatch bought at a roadside stall. The crocodile on the 'Lacoste' polo shirt bought at these markets may 'swim' in the washing machine too. However, garments with fake Chanel, Gucci and Benetton logos make affordable gifts and interesting conversation pieces.

The bazaar-like atmosphere and wide array of goods and bargains reinforces Penang's reputation as a shopping haven. Price haggling adds to the fun and spirit of the night market. Try walking away after making an offer: chances are you will be called back by the vendor. If not, the next stall will carry similar items and the seller will be open to bargaining, which is the name of the game.

Regular night markets are held at the following locations:

Taman Free School: Open ground in the common compound of the low-rise blocks of flats named after it. Both MPPP buses No. 6 and No. 9 will take you there. Board at the Pengkalan Weld terminal or the bus station at KOMTAR.

Gurney: The stretch along the waterfront at the end of **Persiaran Gurney** near the road to Tanjung Tokong. Take the MPPP bus No. 2 which displays the sign 'Bagan Jermal'. Board at the Pengkalan Weld terminal or the bus station at KOMTAR and ride till the end of the route. Once you reach your destination, you will be able to see the colourful lights of the night market as you get down just behind the Sunrise Tower whose ground floor is occupied by McDonald's.

Jalan Johor: Flanks a big football field known as Padang Brown

20 Leith Street

at the end of Jalan Anson. It is across the road from the Penang Buddhist Association. To get there, take MPPP bus No. 1, No. 4 or No. 10 from the Pengkalan Weld terminal or the bus station at KOMTAR. A permanent hawker centre is beside the green near the traffic lights junction with Jalan Perak.

Jalan Sekolah La Salle: Just opposite the Penang State Mosque. Take MPPP bus No. 1 or No. 10 from the Pengkalan Weld Terminal or the bus station at KOMTAR. Alight outside the big mosque along Jalan Air Itam. Cross the road to get to the site. If you are returning to George Town from Air Itam in the evening, you can stop at the night market if it is held there. Behind the area is a densely-populated residential community called the Rifle Range flats, rows of tall buildings which accommodate hundreds of people.

Jalan Ipoh and **Jalan Penaga**: Both near the Jelutong market, a little way out of George Town. This corner has many inexpensive eating places. MPPP bus No. 3 will take you there. Board from the Pengkalan Weld terminal or the bus station at KOMTAR. When you get off at the Jelutong stop, head towards the area lit by fluorescent lights on stakes, a tell-tale sign of the evening market.

Bars and Discos

Sip before you sup; dance the night away, sing karaoke-style, go pub crawling or hibernate on your barstool.

Penang's night haunts and watering holes include pubs, cocktail lounges, karaoke lounges and hotel lobby bars. It is a pretty tame scene by some standards but hardly boring. Major hotels and big restaurants feature live entertainment every evening.

The best spot to nurse a slow drink at sunset is the **Revolving Restaurant** on the 15th floor of the City Bayview Hotel. Take in the panorama of the city as far as the Penang Bridge right across the harbour and the central highlands. The ambience is romantic and the gradual 360-degree rotation at hourly intervals provides ample opportunity to survey George Town at leisure. In the basement level of the hotel is **Keats Pub**, whilst **City Lounge** on the ground floor lobby offers soothing music by a live band.

The **E & O Hotel** behind has a music hall which is a favourite with many sentimental hearts. Nostalgic British songs and popular tunes of the 1940s and 1950s form the repertoire of its resident band which entertains nightly. Dance if you have twinkle toes or just sit back and enjoy the soothing melodies made popular by

singers of yesteryear. If you prefer a quiet evening, the hotel's waterfront promenade has coconut palms which sway in the evening breeze. It is a romantic place by the sea, with the sound of the waves lapping lazily. The **Latin Quarter Night Club** at No. 38-A

Lebuh Farquhar, 150m (163½yds) from the E & O Hotel, has floor shows and cabaret hostesses.

The pub **20 Leith Street**, named after its own address, is across from Cathay Hotel. This nightspot has ample parking space, food stalls and an outdoor beer garden. The bar and darts room are inside the charming 1931 colonial mansion. A deejay spins records from 9pm nightly and there is a small dance floor. Open from 5pm daily for happy hours till 9pm, it closes at 2am on weekdays and at 3am on weekends.

If you pub crawl, head next for the **Hong Kong Bar** at No. 371 Lebuh Chulia. It is easy to spot as trishaws wait outside to take customers home or to supper spots. Sailors and deck hands on shore leave inevitably make a beeline for this place, which has been their haven since the 1950s. Photographs of its patrons plastered all over its walls testify to its international clientele.

Karaoke fans should go to the **Xanadu KTV** in the basement of Hotel Malaysia in No. 7 Jalan Penang. You can sing, if you wish, to the accompaniment of the synthesizer. Opposite it at No. 48A Jalan Penang, **Polar Cafe** has a country and western sing-along with its house organist and music machine nightly. A variety of cocktail and karaoke lounges are found in this same neon-lit area which comes alive at nightfall.

Street One at the mezzanine floor of the Shangri-La Hotel in Jalan Magazine within the KOMTAR Complex is a cosy rendezvous. The **Sri Pinang Lounge** in Merlin Penang at Jalan Larut welcomes crooners who like to perform in public. By day, **Jalan Sultan Ahmad Shah**, formerly known as Northam Road, is George Town's millionaire row. Grand homes constructed at the turn of the century line this raintree-shaded thoroughfare, but its character is fast changing. A proliferation of new clubs and nightspots are now housed in its huge, old mansions which have been converted into snazzy entertainment spots. The brightly-lit **Metropole** has plentiful parking space and offers a bar and karaoke lounge cum nightclub all in one. It closes at 3am on weekends and eves of public holidays. **Hippodrome** at 24 Jalan Sultan Ahmad Shah, opposite the historical Christian graveyard, offers both live and disco music.

Tanjung Tokong on the way to the north coast has a glitzy sunset strip. After dusk, the whole road is ablaze with bright lights and neon signs. **Silverado** is a pub for country and western fans. Right next to it is **The Singles Pub**. The old **Chusan Hotel** has a song and dance nightclub known for its Chinese singers, plus hostesses who will dance with you if you buy them drinks and pay for their time.

Along the same stretch of roads are bars with names like **D'Jockey** and **Sakura**, and **Casablanca,** a lively disco, which is opposite Eden House. New establishments on the scene in Tanjung Tokong are **Diamond Hearts**, a karaoke lounge, and the **New Honeycomb Lounge & Nightclub**, beside the Sin Ming Garden Restaurant.

Further up the road is the **Cartwheel**, located opposite the Chinese Swimming Club in Tanjung Bungah. Park Inn's **Bayu Lounge** is a place to enjoy a refreshing cocktail while its rooftop fun pub, **Night Moves**, features live entertainment all night long.

Shock! Videotheque at Novotel Penang in Tanjung Bungah is where the young and restless enjoy a fast and frantic time. Venture inside for stunning lights, high-energy music and dazzling interiors. The hotel's **Lobby Bar** is for quiet drinks. **Sri Batik Inn** sited on the hillside at 567A Tanjung Bungah provides live music and overlooks the sea.

On the island's north coast in Batu Ferringhi and Teluk Bahang, the beach hotels have their own watering holes for guests. The discotheques open about 9pm and get more crowded a couple of hours later. On weekends, they close at 1 or 2am.

Ozone Bistrotheque at Mar Vista Resort waives cover charge for ladies on Wednesday nights. **Sapphire** discotheque at Ferringhi Beach Hotel is open till 2am on weekdays and closes at 3am on Friday and weekends.

Cinta at the basement of the Rasa Sayang Resort draws a yuppie and youthful crowd. The **Sunset Lounge** at the Golden Sands Resort has a live band which plays dance music nightly and its **Fun Pub** is worth stopping by for a drink. The **Pool Bar** of the Holiday Inn Penang opens from 7.30pm till midnight. **Beers** at the Penang Parkroyal Hotel has large video screens, snooker and darts. **Asmara Lounge** next to the lobby of the Casuarina Beach Hotel features live entertainment in the evenings. **The Study** discotheque at the Mutiara Beach Resort has high-tech electronic gadgets for the fun-loving.

Late Suppers

If hunger pangs grip you after a few drinks, don't worry, food is available till midnight and in some places, all night long.

Post-dinner and pre-midnight feasts are readily available in George Town. Food stalls appear about sunset at **Padang Kota Lama** and they sell a variety of snacks, hot meals, fruits and desserts on the public promenade near the seawall. Opposite the Kuan Yin Teng Temple are some coffeeshops open for the late supper crowd **Loke Kah** at No. 74 Lebuh China straddles two other eating places, **Kwong Soon Lee** and **Kah Pin**. Noodles, fried or served in broth, satay, grilled seafood and yam cake are sold nightly except Sunday.

Lebuh Kimberley, better known as Cheapside, has many roadside hawker stalls sited at the T-junction with Jalan Pintal Tali and Lebuh Cintra. Most dishes are sold out by midnight, especially the duck porridge, fried noodles and the desserts. For a treat, try the hot and sweet almond soup eaten with sliced, crunchy, Chinese deepfried crullers called *yeow char kwai*. Freshly made Malaysian pancakes called *apom* are available too.

Some 150m (163½yds) away is the **Green Planet Restaurant** at No. 63 Lebuh Cintra. This immensely popular foodie's hang-out opens daily till midnight. Many locals and young world travellers gather there to trade travel information and tips while tucking into homemade pies, pizza, spaghetti and sandwiches.

Hsiang Yang Cafe opposite the Tye Ann Hotel and the nearby **Sai Lam** coffee shop at No. 307 Lebuh Chulia have lots of roadside foodstalls at night. Further down the same road, **Tai Wah** coffee shop at No. 487 is thronged nightly with fresh faced tourists from nearby budget hotels enjoying chatter, beer and food.

At **Jalan Penang**, opposite the Cathay cinema, food is available every evening at 'Kris Nite Corner' on the sidewalk of the **Penang Bazaar**. Less than 200m (220yds) to the left of the Chowrasta market are two busy rice shops specialising in hot meals served till dawn. Fish head curry, crabs, pigeon, mutton and other spicy dishes are the specialities of **Kedai Makanan Globe** at No. 4 and **Restoran Chowrasta** at No. 10 Lorong Tamil.

The five-way junction of **Jalan Brick Kiln**, **Jalan Magazine**, **Jalan Datuk Keramat**, **Jalan Macalister** and the end of **Jalan Penang** sees a gathering of hawkers in front of the GAMA department store every night. **Kassim Nasi Kandar**, which never closes, is directly across the road at 2-1 Jalan Brick Kiln. About 100m (110yds) to the right is **Cravan Cafe** at 2 Jalan Datuk Keramat. Both offer a wide range of curries, rice and vegetables.

In Jalan Macalister, **Kedai Kopi Sin Chew Nam** at the New Lane junction has many food vendors in the evening while **Oriental Cafe**, across the road from Wisma Central, is a popular haunt for seafood lovers. Crabs, fish, shrimp and other seafood are baked, steamed or fried. The **Kedai Makanan dan Minuman Low Eng Hoo** at No. 84 Lorong Selamat has a variety of Penang hawker fare. Its *ais kachang* (an icy desert) is quite good. So are the *lobak* or pork roll, deep-fried bean curd and prawn fritters. There are more eating stalls between Jalan Macalister and Jalan Burmah.

At the 2-km (1¼-mile) long coastal stretch called **Pesiaran Gurney**, restaurants, food centres and stalls thrive till the wee hours of the morning. One end has cafes with names such as Carnation, Public and Song River. At the other end, rows and rows of food-stalls are parked outside Sunrise Tower from late afternoon onwards selling anything from freshly-made pizza, burgers and hot dogs, to *laksa* (noodles in spicy fish broth), *rojak* (salad with prawn paste), fruit juices and other mouth-watering temptations.

Jalan Burmah has various food corners. The junction with **Jalan Tavoy** and **Jalan Mandalay** right near the Union Institute is a very busy spot. The variety is mind-boggling. Western meals like chicken chop, steak, fish and chips are available alongside oyster porridge, prawn noodles, soups, vegetable rolls and other Penang delights at **Kedai Kopi Keat Seang**, which closes on Monday, and **Kedai Kopi Cathay**, closed on Sunday. The **Golden Eagle Hawker Centre** at No. 192 Jalan Burmah is also very popular at night.

The area around Lorong Burmah is very active at night too. **Kedai Kopi Kwai Lock** at No. 295-A **Jalan Burmah** tends to be busier in the mornings. On the opposide side of the road are coffeeshops like **Sin Hup Kee** and **Tip Top**. **Kedai Kopi Swee Kong** at the junction with Solok Moulmein, which faces the Pulau Tikus police station sells a variety of foods as do several similar shops further up the road near the traffic junction with Jalan Cantonment. The popular night foodstalls formerly in Gottlieb Road are now relocated at Jalan Pasar, the site of the Pulau Tikus wet market.

There are more eating places at night on both sides of the road at the junction of **Jalan Fettes** with Tanjung Tokong. Try **Fatty Loh Restaurant**, which offers take-out chicken rice in the daytime and an array of other dishes at night. There are other dining spots like the nearby **Kedai Kopi Mun Lam** and the **Tari Burger Cafe** at the start of the Tanjung Tokong seafront promenade. Several Malay hawker centres stretch along the length of this busy thoroughfare which leads to Tanjung Bungah, an area with discos and bars.

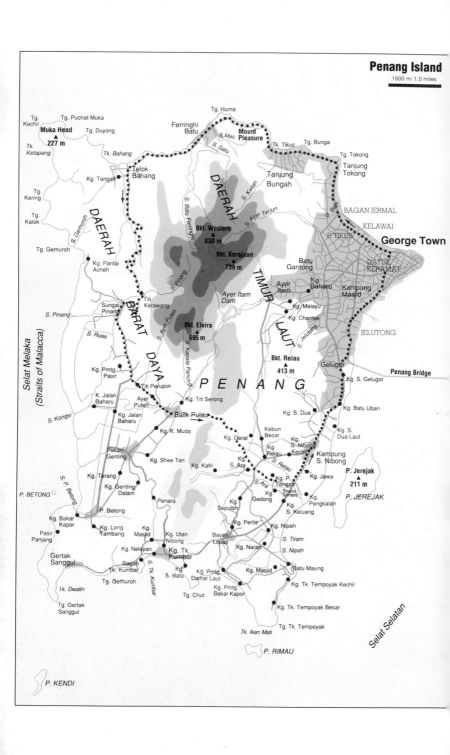

Penang Island

1600 m/ 1,0 miles

Tg. Kechil
Tg. Puchat Muka
Tg. Duyong
Muka Head
227 m
Tk. Ketapang
Tk. Bahang
Kg. Tengah
Telok Bahang
Tg. Kering
Tg. Kalok
Tg. Gemuroh

Ferringhi Batu
Tg. Huma
S. Mas
Mount Pleasure
S. Satu
Tk. Tikus
Tg. Bunga
Tg. Tokong
Tanjung Tokong

DAERAH
S. Kelian
S. Ayer Terjun
Tanjung Bungah

BAGAN JERMAL
KELAWAI
P. TIKUS
George Town

S. Gemuroh
DAERAH
BARAT
DAYA

S. Batu Ferringhi
Bkt. Western
830 m
Bkt. Kerajaan
739 m
Ayer Itam Dam
S. Pinang
Titi Kerawang
Bkt. Elvira
695 m

DAERAH
TIMUR LAUT

Batu Gantong
Ayer Itam
Kg. Baharu
Kg. Melayu
Kg. Chantek

DATUK KERAMAT
Kampung Masjid

S. Jelutong
JELUTONG

Kg. Pantai Acheh
Sungai Pinang
S. Pinang
S. Rusa

Bkt. Relau
413 m
Gelugor
Kg. S. Gelugor
Penang Bridge

Selat Melaka
(Straits of Malacca)

Kg. Pmtg. Pasir
K. Jalan Baharu
Ayer Puteh
Kg. Jalan Baharu
S. Kongsi

S. Ayer Puteh
S. Kepala Pancht

Titi Perupok
Kg. Titi Serong
Balik Pulau
Kg. K. Muda

PENANG

Kg. S. Dua
Kg. Batu Uban

Kebun Besar
Kg. Relau
Kg. S. Nibong Kechil
Kampung S. Nibong
Kg. S. Dua Laut

Kg. Darat
Kg. Shee Tan
Kg. Kafri
Kg. S. Ara

Pekan Genting
Kg. Terang
Kg. Genting Dalam
Penara
P. Betong

S. P. Betong
P. BETONG

Kg. Bakar Kapor
Pasir Panjang
Kg. Long Tambang
Gertak Sanggul

Kg. Masjid
Kg. Nelayan
Kg. Utan Nibong
Bagan Tk. Kumbar
Kg. Tk. Kumbar

S. Tk. Kumbar
S. Batu
Tk. Kumbar
Tg. Gemuroh
Ik. Dwalin
Tg. Gertak Sanggul

Kg. Pmtg. Damar Laut
Kg. Pmtg. Bakar Kapor
Tg. Chut

S. Relau
Kg. P. Tengah
Snake Temple
Kg. Jawa
P. Jerejak
211 m
P. JEREJAK

Kg. Gedong
Kg. Sepuloh
Kg. Pengkalan
Kg. S. Keluang
Kg. Perlis
Kg. Nipah
S. Tiram
S. Nipah
Bayan Lepas
Kg. Naran

Kg. Masjid
Batu Maung
Kg. Tk. Tempoyak Kechil
Kg. Tk. Tempoyak Besar
Tg. Tk. Tempoyak
Tk. Ikan Mati

Selat Selatan

P. RIMAU

P. KENDI

Day TRIPS

6. Circling the Island

Follow the road around the whole isle; stop at various spots of interest; sample local tropical fruits; lunch at Balik Pulau's market; head back to George Town via the coastal strip.

This 80-km (50-mile) journey through the countryside goes past beaches, villages, plantations, the airport, factories, Snake Temple, the city and takes in all the sights for a quick feel of the whole island. At least six hours should be set aside for this tour.

Refer to *Day Itinerary 3* to begin this trip which follows an anti-clockwise direction from **George Town** to **Tanjung Tokong**, then the coastal villages of **Tanjung Bungah, Batu Ferringhi** and **Teluk Bahang**. The two-way coastal road winds a lot, so it is advisable not to speed at all.

From Teluk Bahang, outside the mosque after the **Craft Batik** factory, it is 20km (12½ miles) to **Balik Pulau**. Go past the **Green Orchid farm** where orchid lovers should stroll through, then the **Rimba Rekreasi Teluk Bahang Jabatan Hutan** – the Forestry Museum and Arboretum – as well as the **Butterfly Farm**, which are all on the left. A couple of kilometres on is a picnic spot accessible by two steep laterite paths on the right. Cars parked on the grass verge indicate where to leave yours if you are keen to swim in cold

fresh water from the hills. The distance to Balik Pulau is another 17km (10½ miles).

Flanking this road is a dense canopy of vegetation. *Durian* and rubber trees grow on the slopes on the right. The winding road starts to climb up 2km (1¼ miles) further on. Pass by **See Hong Estate**, a nutmeg farm on the right. On dry days, trays of nutmeg fruit and mace are left under the sun outside the farmhouse. Cross one of the many small bridges that ford the river heading downstream.

At about the 12-km (7½-mile) road marker (towards Balik Pulau), there is a flower nursery on the right. After this, the **Titi Kerawang Stall** at the 11-km (6¾-mile) point is a fine rest stop. The valley down below has coconut and rubber plantations. Besides the scenic views, you can buy local fruits and drinks, T-shirts and souvenirs at the stall.

One kilometre further down are more souvenir stores selling similar items. Just five minutes away on foot to the left, a cool waterfall cascades into a pool; watch out for slippery rocks if you want to swim. Take a break in the shade or have a picnic under the trees.

As you continue, the road slopes down. A good landmark is the **Sungei Pinang Reservoir**, a big, white, round concrete container behind a high wire fence which is 7km (4¼ miles) to Balik Pulau. The reservoir signboard warns against trespassing.

After the reservoir, you will pass by **Sungei Pinang** village whose police station is on the left side of the road. It lies 6km (3¼ miles) from Balik Pulau and on the way there, you will go past **Sungei Rusa** village, which has lovely wooden houses on stilts and well-swept compounds. Then, you come to **Permatang Pasir** village, located some 2km (1¼ miles) down the road.

Keep going straight on past the **Jalan Permatang Pasir** junction and **Seng Motor**, a car repair garage and body shop. The road turns right into **Jalan Baru** but you want to veer left towards **Titi Teras** village which has a little stream of the same name about 2km (1¼ miles) from Balik Pulau. Travel past the **Tanako garment factory** which is just before the **Balik Pulau fire station**. A Chinese graveyard is on the left, followed by a Hindu temple, the town magistrate court and a district hospital.

At the lamp light fountain, which has water gushing out of lion heads, you enter the Main Road of **Balik Pulau**. The Penang Yellow Bus Station is behind it. About 150m (163⅓yds) down the street to the left is the market which will have many people milling outside it. Several hawker stalls here sell noodles, vegetables and pork rolls and other cooked foods worth sampling.

This is a good place to stop for a well-deserved lunch. Try Kim's *laksa* (spicy fish noodle soup) in a coffee shop called **Lam Kong**, No. 67 Main Road. For a wider lunch choice, look for **Kedai Kopi Green Garden** at No. 73 located after Ban Lee (No. 69), a broom maker's shop, and Kedai Runcit Kee Seng, a grocery, at No. 71 Main Road. Across the road from the market is **Sin Chuan Heang** at No. 104 and **Kedai Makanan Meng Heong** at No. 114.

After lunch, continue your

Malay kampung house

Balik Pulau

round-island drive. Exit right at the end of Main Road after the market and you will find **Jalan Relau** which connects with **Jalan Tun Sardon**. The latter climbs steeply up as it was cut through the hills. The scenery is spectacular until you head downhill. At the fork road ahead, turn right to **Bayan Lepas** to get to the Snake Temple.

The **Snake Temple** or the **Temple of Azure Cloud**, is dedicated to the deity Chor Soo Kong. Many souvenir shops can be found outside the temple while inside, you will find poisonous Wagler's pit vipers. These green and yellow serpents feed on hen eggs supplied by devotees. Look for them in the main hall. There is a warning sign advising visitors not to touch the snakes.

Go in further to the second hall on the left. There, professional photographers wait with de-venomed snakes which they offer to drape around your shoulders or on your head like Medusa, and take a snapshot. Try to smile, even if if you feel like grimacing. If you use your own camera, just pay the photographer RM2. It costs RM16 if the photographer uses his own equipment for your snapshot – the price includes sending the processed photos by registered post to your home address. Remember to write your name and full mailing address on the envelope provided.

In the open garden at the back of the temple are plants and some good spots for photography. Inside the wall enclosure are mango trees where you will often see some more vipers camouflaged among the branches and leaves. To com-

Snake Temple

plete your round-island tour, go back to George Town via Jalan Jelutong. You will pass Penang Bridge on your right.

Ways to Do Your Round Island Tour

1) Rent a car: just follow the main route which has regular kilometre markers and keep to the tarred roads. Avoid dirt tracks and other secondary paths. There are signs pointing to major towns along the way.

2) Hire a taxi or limousine: most hotels provide limo services. The driver will double as a guide and will give you personal insights into the way of life in the region. An air-conditioned limousine costs RM90 per half-day and RM150 for a full-day tour. Taxi rates are slightly less, but bargain first. Either will accommodate up to four passengers per car, excluding the chauffeur.

3) A guided coach tour: for RM40, this is available at all hotels and tour counters. An escort gives a running commentary as the coach whizzes by the rural areas. Stops are made at various places of interest, including the Snake Temple.

4) Public transport: to get to the Snake Temple, board the Penang Yellow Bus No. 66 at the **Pengkalan Weld** bus terminus for RM1.10 to the temple at **Sungei Kluang**. Stop after the Interquartz and Cybiotronis factories on the left side of the road. The temple is across the road. The journey lasts about 40 minutes. After visiting the temple, board the next No. 66 service and pay RM1.30 to get to Balik Pulau, which offers a glimpse of what George Town was like 30 to 50 years ago. Here, explore the market, enjoy lunch and see the town. But make sure you keep track of time as you want to continue on to **Teluk Bahang**. Penang Yellow Bus No. 76 will take you there from Balik Pulau. Board at the bus terminal near the town fountain on Main Road. There is an interval of two hours between buses and the last bus leaves at 7.15pm. The fare is RM1.20 for the hour-long journey.

Once you get to Teluk Bahang, catch the Hin Bus at the village roundabout to go downtown via Batu Ferringhi. The fare is RM1.40 and the journey goes via the northern coastline. Try and get a seat on the seafacing side to catch views of ravines, isolated beaches, palm trees and houses. You can alight anywhere en route. To get back to George Town, change buses at the **Tanjung Bungah** station before the last bus departs at midnight for the ferry terminus.

7. Central Penang

Visit Air Itam in the centre of Penang. Browse in its bustling daily morning market; climb up to an immense temple and a dam sited behind it; have lunch in the village; then take a tram up Penang Hill and dine under the stars with glittering George Town down below.

Air Itam: If you are starting from George Town, go to the city bus terminus opposite the ferry terminal and take MPPP bus No. 1 right to the end of its run at **Air Itam** village in front of a cakeshop. After you alight, you may want to try the cakeshop's freshly-baked cinnamon buns which are very popular among the locals.

Walk across to the market 100m (110yds) ahead to the left. You will see some stalls with a profusion of tropical fruits. Piles of pineapples and watermelons are laid out on the ground and bunches of bananas dangle down from hooks. You can always return later to buy some. Imported grapes, oranges, apples and pears are also on display. When in season, there will be mangoes and other local fruits like *rambutans, mangosteens, langsats* and *durians*.

From the market, proceed another 100m (110yds) past shophouses to the left and wooden houses on the right. When you arrive at the car park after the shops, bear left. Go straight by a row of souvenir stores and over a bridge under which flows a stream with bamboo clumps on its banks. This is the way up to the **Kek Lok Si temple**, which was completed in 1904.

This is the largest Buddhist temple complex in Malaysia. Pilgrims ascend via the granite steps and up a covered arcade full of shops. The shopowners will beckon you to look at their imitation Lacoste, Chanel and Dior garments. Lucky charms, wind chimes, statuettes and other decorative items are laid out on shelves and tables. If you wish to buy anything, do so on the way down so as not to be laden

Kek Lok Si Temple, pagoda and roof

Ornate Kek Lok Si Temple

with purchases on the way up.

After five minutes of climbing, you reach the hall of Bodhisattvas, which is the first part of the temple. Dedicated to Kuan Yin, the Goddess of Mercy, her statue is enshrined in a grotto tableau behind the altar table. A nun attends the counter selling incense and candles. She hands out a slip of paper on which is written an ancient verse to correspond with the fortune-telling stick that pilgrims have selected. It is customary to make a small cash contribution if she explains and interprets the message for you.

On the next level, you pass by a big tortoise pond. Devotees release these creatures to earn blessings in life. Here, you can buy vegetables and biscuits to feed the tortoises or cold drinks to quench your thirst. A large fish pond with swimming carp is found on the next terrace.

The plants and flowers make this spot ideal for photography. To the right is a stall with Chinese imperial costumes for hire. Here you can dress up as a Ming emperor and have a snapshot taken if

you do not have a camera with you. The photographer there can create 'special effects' and the resultant picture may depict you flying in the air or holding the temple on your outstretched palm!

Huge boulders on the right of the upward bound staircase are inscribed with Chinese verses. The calligraphy works are extracts from Confucian texts, Buddhist scriptures and late Ching dynasty poetry works. Readers of the language will have a field day looking at the chiselled inscriptions.

At the top of the flight of steps is an arched doorway, and beyond that a pavil-

ion with multiple Buddha figures. Turn right to the hall of Devas, the four kings whom Buddhists believe guard the north, south, east and west gates of heaven. They are encased in glass and below their feet are representatives of the wicked – a drunkard, an opium addict, a prostitute and a gambler – who are prevented from going to heaven.

The portly gilded statue of the laughing Buddha, Maitreya, who

Kek Lok Si Temple

symbolises happiness, is on a raised table. Pilgrims offer flowers, fruits and incense on the altar in front of Maitreya in the hope of gaining favours. On the far right, in an alcove, is the statue of Confucius. Parents bring their children here to pray for guidance and inspiration in studies.

The next hall is devoted to Sakyamuni Buddha and has three great statues. The founder of Buddhism is in the centre. Ananda, his favourite disciple, is on the left and Kasyapa, another disciple, is on the right. Lined up against the walls around the same room are 18 statues of *lohans*, who are believed to have foresight and can foretell the future.

Exit left and down a short stairway to where the monastery is found. Go up the long flight of steps in front to arrive at the landing where the seven-tier tower which incorporates Chinese, Thai and Burmese architecture stands. Make a donation to climb this pagoda of 10,000 Buddhas. You can walk up to the lower roof level from where you can see the foothill village of Air Itam and vegetable farms on the slopes.

After you have toured the temple, if you are not too tired and can wait a little for lunch, you might want to go to the **Air Itam Dam** located behind the temple. This is a jogging and exercise spot. People walk or jog up and down the sloping roads which rise to 71m (233ft) above sea level. The route, which begins right at the back of the Kek Lok Si Temple, is 3-km (1¾-miles) long but seems longer as you will be going uphill all the time. The gardens surrounding the dam are neat and well kept. It is a quiet and restful public recreational park. You can see the water level in the open, uncovered, man-made lake of the dam site. The park is open from 4.30pm to 7.30pm on weekdays and Saturdays; 6.30am to 9am on Sundays.

Then, return to the temple and descend the same way you came up. Back on the ground, turn left after the bridge crossing and seek

View from Penang Hill

out **Chooi Lim Koo**, an old restaurant which serves good local food. You can also eat at the many coffeeshops near the bridge.

Penang Hill: After lunch, walk back to the cakeshop in Air Itam village centre. Board the MPPP bus No. 8 which will take you to the station at the foot of Penang Hill. There are plenty of taxis at this spot which you can take to return to your hotel afterwards.

Alternatively, take a five-minute taxi ride from Air Itam to the Lower Station of Penang Hill Railway. Ascend Penang Hill, once the exclusive domain of the rich and originally opened in the mid-1800s for the convalescence of tired minds and bodies. Its invigorating air is conducive for rest, recreation and relaxation and an escape from lowland heat.

The **funicular railway** which was started in 1923 makes the summit of Penang Hill accessible to the public. This engineering feat ended the pony riding and palanquin travel which necessitated servants carrying their masters uphill in sedan chairs.

The cable car fare costs RM4 return for adults and RM2 for children. The half-hour journey each way in the Swiss-made cars by-passes various stations and enters a tunnel before arriving at the top.

The earliest train up departs at 6.30am daily. The last journey down from the top is at 9.15pm, except on Thursday, Saturday and Sunday, when there is a 'midnight' run at 11.45pm For charter rates, please call 683-263.

Uphill living at Bukit Bendera (as Penang Hill is now called), is 700m (2,300ft) above sea level, amidst nature's beauty.

Portfolio of the special effects photographer

There are many holiday bungalows and private homes on the hill. **Bel Retiro**, the governor's hilltop residence, was built by convict labour some 150 years ago. English-style houses like Edgecliff, Woodside and Southview which have stone walls, wooden floors, fireplaces, chimneys and gardens are rented out for quiet vacations.

The tea kiosk above the top station of the hill railway serves tea and cold drinks to tired hikers. Most visitors frequent the hawker centre which has stalls selling food and beverages. There are also some souvenir shops. Nearby are a police station and a post office which are adjacent to each other. A mosque and a Hindu temple are sited on a ridge behind the bazaar.

Nearby is the 12-room **Bellevue Hotel** (Tel: 699-500), which has well-tended flower gardens and an aviary with rare hornbills and other tropical birds.

The restaurant has lovely art on its walls to go with your tea or meals. The lawn in front has a stunning, sweeping view of George Town below, which sparkles with lights at night.

After an afternoon of walking exploring the summit and enjoying the fresh, unpolluted air, have a quiet and pleasant meal in the restaurant's hall or on the balcony which is covered by a trellis creeping with jade plants.

There are many **walking trails** on Penang Hill which lead to homes on **Tiger Hill**, **Fern Hill** and **Western Hill**. A well-beaten path runs all the way down to the base of Penang Hill. It ends at Moon Gate just before the Botanical Gardens (see *Pick & Mix Itinerary 8*). The high altitude and cooler climate supports the rich flora and fauna.

With prior arrangement, the taxi you booked before you went up Penang Hill will be waiting to take you back to your hotel.

8. Trekking

Pack your knapsack: bring along a compass, a flask of drinking water and food, put on your walking shoes and hit the trail.

Adventurous walks for the energetic are recommended. Some suggested trails include:

Pantai Acheh forest reserve: Located northwest of the island, the trek to this 2,000-hectare (5,000-acre) nature reserve is deserted but well marked. Begin from the beach after the highrise block of flats in Teluk Bahang. Take a taxi there from your hotel but remember to negotiate with

The trek to Pantai Acheh Reserve

Beach at the start of Pantai Acheh Reserve Trek

the driver to take you back to your hotel at the end of the day.

Keracut beach and park: Rewards those who reach the end of the two-hour long trail. It can be wet and slippery after a rainfall. Walk carefully along the well-trodden paths. Remember to have on good, comfortable walking shoes with soles that grip well.

A marine research and biological field station run by Universiti Sains Malaysia is the only sign of civilisation there. Several bungalows are located further away. Instead of hiking, you could arrange for a fishing boat from the jetty at Kampung Medan Nelayan in Teluk Bahang to send you to Teluk Aling at the site of the marine research centre and which forms part of the nature reserve – and pick you up later.

Muka Head: This is a lighthouse which signals that land ahoy is at the extreme northwest tip of Penang. Hiking is most challenging there. The three-hour trek from Kampung Medan Nelayan is quite an obstacle course if you are not fit. The undulating route involves balancing across drain pipes and pole walkways. The scenery is lush, green and wild. It is a popular hike for school kids and youth groups.

Penang Hill: This trek on foot takes about four hours. About half the time is needed for going down. Start from the **Moon Gate** near the **Botanical Gardens**. Follow the well-trodden hiking path. It is rocky and laterite-covered in parts. As you near the end, there is a tarred road that leads to the summit before emerging near the Bellevue Hotel.

An alternative trail is a tarred road frequently used by four-wheel drive jeeps that winds up to Penang Hill.

A fisherman waits for passengers at the Kampung Medan Nelayan Jetty

It begins beside the main entrance to the Botanical Gardens. The ascent is scenic and lovely, but this route gets rather crowded on weekends with morning walkers pacing up and down.

Tiger Hill: Sounds exciting but belies the fact that big cats prowl no more in Penang. The climb is steep but not arduous. The road leads to Western Hill, the highest spot for hiking. There is Mother Nature in all her glory to admire along the way back and forth.

Air Itam Dam: Has a trail to **Sungei Pinang**. About 50m (54½yds) from the playground is a stony track that runs uphill and later downhill, meadering through spice and fruit orchards. During the *durian* season, watch out for the falling spiked fruits. The final destination is the waterfall at Titi Kerawang, a place for a refreshing dip to cool off and picnic. Crystal-clear water flows down from the hills and falls into a big pool. The rocky surroundings are often wet and slippery. Several stalls on the main road sell drinks, edibles and souvenirs. It is very popular during weekends and public holidays.

9. Across the Channel

Pack a picnic basket; drive or take the ferry to Butterworth; visit the Penang Bird Park; trek and have a picnic at the Bukit Mertajam Forest Recreation Park.

The ferry ride between the island (Pengkalan Weld, George Town) and the mainland is a great bargain. Adults pay 40 sen and children under 12 years only 20 sen. You pay just once on boarding in Butterworth and not from Penang. On board the double-decker boats which are named after major Malaysian islands, you can enjoy the sea breeze while crossing the narrow channel. The journey is 20 minutes each way.

Penang Bridge

Lush aviary at the Bird Park

There are two types of ferries: some solely for vehicles and others which carry passengers as well. They run all day but only at half hourly intervals after midnight. Cars with engines from 1,201 to 1,600 cc are charged RM7. Peak rush hours are during early morning and late afternoon.

Alternatively, you can drive across the 13½-km (8½-mile) **Penang Bridge**, the longest in Southeast Asia. Its central portion is tall enough for ships to pass under. At night, the bridge becomes ablaze with lights. A toll of RM7 is collected from each vehicle going to the island. Vehicular traffic crossing back from Penang to the mainland of Peninsular Malaysia are not charged. The bridge is out of bounds to pedestrians and cyclists.

Another way of doing this itinerary is by hiring a cab in Penang for about RM15 per hour or RM60 for half a day as this tour takes at least five hours to complete.

In **Butterworth**, the **Penang Bird Park** is at **Taman Tunku** in Seberang Jaya, a 10-minute drive or 7km (4¼ miles) from the Penang Bridge toll plaza. From the Butterworth ferry terminal, it is 12km (7½ miles) away.

Get there by following this route: Jalan Chain Feri, Jalan Baru, Jalan Tun Hussein Onn, Jalan Jelawat and the turn left into Jalan Todak. Bus No. 65 from the Central Province Wellesley Transport Company at the Butterworth bus station leaves for the big park hourly. On the first floor of the public bus terminal are eating stalls if you want a simple local meal of noodles or rice. There is also a supermarket if you wish to buy food, fruits and drinks for a picnic hamper to take along to Bukit Mertajam. Taxis are parked on the ground floor and will transport passengers to points beyond Butterworth.

The bird park is set in a lush green garden, a nature spot showcasing some 200 avian species from Malaysia and other parts of the

world in captivity. The 2-ha (5-acre) grounds also have ponds with water-fowl, fish and water plants. Pelicans and swans roam freely in the open. Two aviaries are designed as geodesic domes. A huge aviary allows visitors to walk amidst flying birds, including multi-coloured lories, macaws and parrots.

Landscape gardening has added ornamental vegetation such as the cacti, palms and bamboo. Collections of orchid and hibiscus hybrids are carefully tended. Water lilies thrive in the ponds filled with Japanese carp. The bird park also houses a children's playground, a souvenir shop and a restaurant.

Entry charge is RM3 per adult and RM1 for children under 12 years. It costs RM10 for each video camera taken in. Parking is free for coaches and cars. Guided tours can be arranged for groups. Opening hours are from 9am to 7pm. The final admission is half an hour before the closing time, Tel: 391-899.

From the bird park, drive or catch a taxi to the **Bukit Mertajam Forest Recreation Park**, a refreshingly cool area which lies between the towns of Kulim and Bukit Mertajam. The park is home to a natural rainforest, 500m (1,640ft) above sea level and remains as one of the rare pockets of natural rain forest in Penang.

The trees here consist of *Meranti rambai daun* (*Shorea acuminata*), *Seraya* (*Shorea curtisii*) *Kelat* (*Eugenia*) and *Kedondong* (*Dacryodes*). A variety of ferns, epiphytes and wild flowers form a secondary forest carpet on the ground. Crystal clear streams with small waterfalls flow down the hill slopes.

There are some jungle tracks within this forest. Walking along the tracks offers chance encounters with insects, birds and butterflies. The tracks rejoin the main tarred road mid-way to the summit where a microwave station is situated. On the way up, there are two platforms with panoramic views of the forest and its surroundings. Small pools along the river contain cool water; its banks making good picnic grounds.

From Bukit Mertajam, the park is about 2km (1¼ miles) on the way to Kulim. A bus service runs from Butterworth to Bukit Mertajam and to Kulim every 15 minutes. The fare from Bukit Mertajam is only 30 sen. The service begins at 6am and ends at midnight. Taxis are available either from Butterworth, Bukit Mertajam or Kulim.

After this, catch another taxi to **Mengkuang Valley**, north of Bukit Mertajam. The biggest

Mengkuang Valley Dam

dam in Penang, it can hold 23,639 million litres of fresh water. There are landscaped grounds, recreational and sporting facilities, jogging tracks and walking trails. Seek permission from the security guards before entering as water catchment areas like this are well protected and some areas are not open to the public.

Bukit Mertajam town attracts many Roman Catholic pilgrims during the mid-year Saint Anne's Feast, held annually on 26 July. The people throng the place to offer prayers to the mother of Virgin Mary for nine days. Two street processions take place on 26 and 29 July. A candlelight mass, attended by hundreds of followers, is held at midnight on 30 July, which marks the end of the novena.

To get to Bukit Mertajam, after crossing the Penang Bridge, follow the signboards that read '**Butterworth**'. Then, bear left on **Highway 1** that points to 'Bukit Mertajam'. At the roundabout in front, make a semi-circle turn and continue 3½km (2 miles) past the Petronas and Shell service stations into the town.

When you reach the traffic lights, a post office is on the left. Turn left and go 500m (545yds) till you see the police station on the right. There is a clock tower on its right – turn towards it. You should be behind the police station.

Proceed for another 500m (545yds), pass stores on both sides of the road and turn right. Ahead of you is the Mobil station. Turn left into **Jalan Kulim** and go straight till you pass the Bukit Mertajam hospital on the

St Anne's Church

right and the St Marguerite's convent school beside it. Another 500m (545yds) down on the right is the new, white **St Anne's Church**, which is the centre of attention when mass and prayer services are held during the St Anne's Feast.

Still on Jalan Kulim and about 1km (½ mile) down on the left is the older, historic church – also called St Anne's Church – which was originally established in 1846. Constructed in French Gothic architectural style, it has been newly restored. A centre for prayer, worship and pilgrimage, it is open from 7am to 7pm daily.

After this excursion on the mainland of Peninsular Malaysia, drive or cab back across the bridge to Penang island.

Eating Out

Eating is a national pastime among Malaysians. And Penangites know this only too well. If you have come to the island to eat, you are in good company. The Penangite's passion for food never abates, and is almost insatiable. Penang's reputation as a gourmet's mecca is well known, from its rough-and-tumble road-side vendors to glitzy, up-market restaurants. Interestingly, Penang cuisine is often promoted abroad at leading hotels through events like Penang Food Week.

Penang cuisine is an interesting melange of local fare, borrowing the best from Malaysia's multi-racial community. Malay food usually consists of rice eaten with curries. *Sambal*, a spicy condiment of pounded chilli, onions and tamarind, is served with beef, fish, prawn and vegetable dishes. And of course, *satay* dipped in a spicy peanut dip is known throughout the world.

Peranakan-style meals on the other hand are a blend of Chinese and Malay cooking methods using local spices and herbs. The best is traditionally prepared using a granite mortar and pestle, or a grinding block to turn coriander, peppercorn and chillies into a paste with dried shrimps and other ingredients.

Chinese food in Penang ranges from simple Hainanese chicken rice to spicy Szechuan dishes. Early migrants from China introduced the subtleties of Cantonese, Hokkien, Hakka, Teochew and Shang-

Dim Sum restaurant

hainese cuisine. The result is a rich and exciting array of culinary delights. With bountiful waters surrounding the island, the Chinese have also developed an entire cuisine around seafood.

If you are a non-meat eater, Chinese vegetarian food will appeal. Many items are made to resemble fish, chicken and pork. For instance, yam is cooked and moulded to look like fish; soya bean curd is fashioned into chicken drumsticks; and gluten becomes mock pork. If looks are deceptive, then this genre of food certainly takes the cake.

Indian cuisine is available in many speciality restaurants serving authentic Indian dishes using aromatic spices. Many curries are spicy hot and pungent, although some, especially the North Indian variety, are less fiery. *Korma* dishes tend to be milder still, though full of flavour.

In addition to the foods of Malaysia's main racial groups, you will find an array of speciality restaurants serving Japanese, Thai and western food.

Recommended Restaurants

If you have acquired a taste for life's finest pleasures, especially lip-smacking victuals and superb fare, the kitchens of Penang's homes are definitely worth investigating. Without a proper invitation however, the next best solution is to try recommended dishes in restaurants. For suggestions on where to try Penang hawker-fare, see the *Nightlife* chapter.

The following list, although not exhaustive, is a useful guide on where to eat the best of different cuisines. As a general guide, a meal without drinks per person is categorised as such: Inexpensive = less than RM10; Moderate = RM10–RM25; Expensive = RM25 and above. As most big restaurants add a 10 percent service charge to the bill, extra tipping is no longer necessary except when exceptional attention and service is accorded.

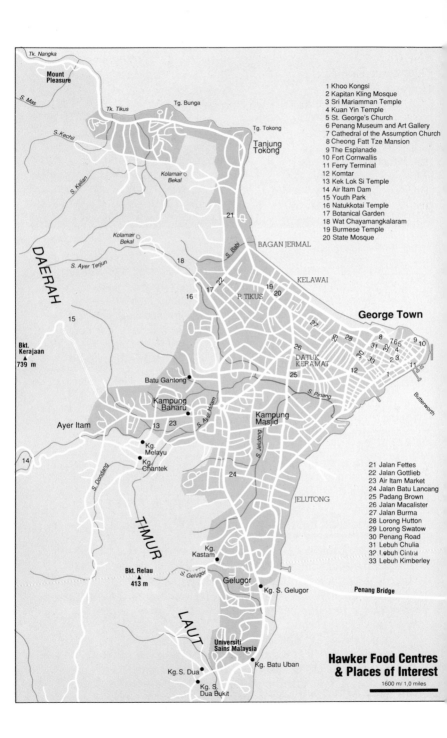

1 Khoo Kongsi
2 Kapitan Kling Mosque
3 Sri Mariamman Temple
4 Kuan Yin Temple
5 St. George's Church
6 Penang Museum and Art Gallery
7 Cathedral of the Assumption Church
8 Cheong Fatt Tze Mansion
9 The Esplanade
10 Fort Cornwallis
11 Ferry Terminal
12 Komtar
13 Kek Lok Si Temple
14 Air Itam Dam
15 Youth Park
16 Natukkotai Temple
17 Botanical Garden
18 Wat Chayamangkalaram
19 Burmese Temple
20 State Mosque

21 Jalan Fettes
22 Jalan Gottlieb
23 Air Itam Market
24 Jalan Batu Lancang
25 Padang Brown
26 Jalan Macalister
27 Jalan Burma
28 Lorong Hutton
29 Lorong Swatow
30 Penang Road
31 Lebuh Chulia
32 Lebuh Cintra
33 Lebuh Kimberley

Tk. Nangka
Mount Pleasure
S. Mas
S. Kechil
Tk. Tikus
Tg. Bunga
Tg. Tokong
Tanjung Tokong
DAERAH
S. Kelian
Kolamair Bekal
Kolamair Bekal
S. Ayer Terjun
BAGAN JERMAL
S. Babi
KELAWAI
George Town
P. TIKUS
Bkt. Kerajaan 739 m
Batu Gantong
Kampung Baharu
Ayer Itam
Kg Melayu
Kg Chantek
DATUK KERAMAT
S. Pinang
Kampung Masjid
S. Ayer Itam
S. Jelutong
S. Dondang
Butterworth
JELUTONG
TIMUR
Bkt. Relau 413 m
Kg. Kastam
S. Gelugor
Gelugor
Kg. S. Gelugor
Penang Bridge
LAUT
Universiti Sains Malaysia
Kg. Batu Uban
Kg.S. Dua
Kg. S. Dua Bukit

Hawker Food Centres & Places of Interest

1600 m/ 1,0 miles

Malay

ELIZA
City Bayview Hotel
25-A Lebuh Farquhar, George Town
Tel: 633-161
Village-style cuisine using authentic spices and fresh herbs. The classical sounds of a *dondang asli* band entertain diners with favourite Malay melodies. Superb views of George Town from this 14th floor level. Open for lunch and dinner daily, including public holidays; closed for dinner on Monday.
Moderate to *Expensive*

MINAH
362-S Sungei Gelugor
Bukit Gelugor
Tel: 881-234
Delicious home-style Malay cooking in unpretentious surroundings. Choose from an array of ready-cooked dishes or order a la carte from the kitchen. *Inexpensive*

PAPA DIN BAMBOO
Behind Restoran Happy Garden
Batu Ferringhi Village
No telephone
Walk in for a native-style dining experience. Popular with foreign travellers who relish sampling local food in a simple, unfussy place. Traditional massage and medicine available too. *Inexpensive*

TAMBUAH MAS
Level 4, KOMTAR
Jalan Penang, George Town
Tel: 622-221
Serves Indonesian/Malaysian cuisine above Pizza Hut joint in a huge shopping complex. Its daily buffet lunch is good value for money and the a la carte menu is also available. Open daily from 11am to 11pm.
Moderate

WANCIK LAZIM
DG-9 Tanjung Tokong
Tel: 895-588
Situated on the ground floor corner lot of a block of government-built flats near the Tanjung Tokong seaside promenade. Spicy, sumptuous curries for those who love it red-hot. *Inexpensive*

SEROJA CAFE
Holiday Inn, Batu Ferringhi
Tel: 811-601
Traditional Malay food served in a modern hotel setting.
Moderate to *Expensive*

Peranakan

DRAGON KING
99 Lebuh Bishop, George Town
Tel: 618-035
A menu of *Peranakan* favourites the way grandma used to make them. Go early at noontime to avoid waiting in line for a table. A more relaxed place in the evening. *Moderate*

SIN KHEANG AUN
2 Lorong Chulia, George Town
Tel: 614-786
Its ordinary coffee shop ambience belies its excellent food. Recommended dishes include the *assam* fish curry, prawn *kerabu*, curry chicken *kapitan* and *tanghoon* soup. *Moderate*

NEW SEAVIEW VILLAGE
(SIN HAI KHENG)
551 Tanjung Bungah
Tel: 806-229
Seaside terrace dining with a good range of *Peranakan* dishes, satay and seafood. Try the spring rolls and fried noodles. *Moderate*

LONE PINE RESTAURANT
Batu Ferringhi
Tel: 811-511

Enjoy eating from tiffin on the lawn by the seaside. The Sunday buffet lunch spread offers a delectable variety of dishes. *Moderate*

Nyonya Corner
15 Jalan Pahang, George Town
Tel: 281-412
Traditional *Peranakan* restaurant run by Yong Chooi Im, a 4th generation *nyonya* (*Peranakan* lady). The charming restaurant is cosily housed in a colonial bungalow with Chinese antique furniture and heirloom ceramics. Open from 11.30am–3pm and from 6.30–10pm Tuesday to Sunday. *Moderate*

Seafood

Eden Seafood Village
69-A Batu Ferringhi
Tel: 811-852
Aquariums with live fish, lobster and shrimp greet customers at this huge restaurant. A cultural performance comes on nightly to entertain diners. Frequented by many tourists. *Moderate* to *Expensive*

End Of The World
(Ah Sim Seafood)
Kampung Nelayan, Teluk Bahang
Tel: 811-189
This simple-looking restaurant is often packed. Best to phone ahead and place your orders before going. The restaurant owes its unusual name to its location at the extreme end of the northwest bay. *Moderate*

Hai Choo Hooi
338 Tanjung Tokong
Tel: 894-375
A restaurant with an outdoor setting in a fishing settlement away from the main road. Great place to eat chilli crabs. *Moderate*

Maple Garden
99 Jalan Penang, George Town
Tel: 635-886
For those who like seafood cooked Chinese style. Located conveniently in the heart of town with a taxi stand outside. *Moderate*

Ocean Green
99 Jalan Peneng, George Town
Tel: 635-886
Sea-facing terrace restaurant at the old Paramount Hotel. An a la carte menu offers seafood dishes, steamboat and seafood congee. Open from noon till 11pm. *Moderate*

Sea Palace
50 Jalan Penang, George Town
Tel: 635-146/633-331
Malaysian-Chinese restaurant in central George Town near various hotels and night haunts. *Moderate*

Tasty Aquaculture
3 Lebuh Raya Batu Maung
Tel: 837-651
Dine under the stars on finger-licking good seafood on the pier. A boatman rows out to bring in the fish and crabs from traps in the sea. Often called 'the beginning of the world', phone reservations are necessary and only accepted in the morning before 1pm. Closed on Wednesday. *Moderate*

THE CATCH
1 Teluk Bahang
Mutiara Beach Resort, Telok Bahang
Tel: 812-828
Sumptuous food amidst unique Malaysian setting and decor. A stage show features national folk dances during mealtimes. *Expensive*

YUYI SEAFOOD
48-01 Taman Indah
Jalan Hassan Abas, Teluk Bahang
Tel: 812-146 (7am to 3.30pm)
Located on the corner ground floor of a block of flats in Kampung Nelayan. Sit on chairs in the pavement or under the trees outside. Open for business from 5–11pm daily and orders accepted by phone earlier. *Inexpensive*

Chinese

CHUAN LOCK HOOI
1-E &1-F Jalan Macalister
George Town
Tel: 371-171
Specialises in Hokkien-style dishes like braised eel, fried vermicelli and glass noodles, yam duck and beancurd. *Moderate*

DRAGON INN
27-B Jalan Gottlieb, George Town
Tel: 379-049
A small restaurant with only a few tables offering very delicious Chinese dishes. *Moderate* to *Expensive*

PROSPEROUS
25-C Jalan Gottlieb
George Town
Tel: 378-787
Traditional Chinese and local Malaysian meals served at this restaurant frequented by people celebrating weddings, birthdays and other joyous occasions. *Moderate*

HOUSE OF FOUR SEASONS
Mutiara Beach Resort, Teluk Bahang
Tel: 812-828
Classy restaurant with Chinese decor, nice atmosphere and quality food. Fancy place to entertain. Try its regular Sunday morning *dim sum. Expensive*

HOLLYWOOD
543 Tanjung Bungah
Tel: 807-269
Enjoy lunch and dinner under trees by the coast. Recommended are the

A friendly neighbourhood bread seller

spring rolls, baked crab and noodles. *Moderate*

NEW METROPOLE RESTAURANT
46 Jalan Sultan Ahmad Shah
George Town
Tel: 366-330
Dine in a huge mansion along Penang's Millionaires' Row.
Moderate

SUPERTANKER
KOMTAR, Jalan Penang, George Town
Tel: 616-393
Teochew food at its best but has other Chinese-style dishes. Popular with businessmen for entertaining clients. *Expensive*

SHANG PALACE
Shangri-La Hotel, George Town
Tel: 622-622
Cantonese stir-fried and steamed cuisine amidst elegant setting. Pricey but delicious *dim-sum* for breakfast and at lunchtime.
Expensive

Chinese Vegetarian

HAPPY REALM
223-B Jalan Burmah, George Town
Tel: 71-918
Besides serving hot meals, this restaurant has shelves of vegetarian goodies on sale. *Moderate*

PHOE THAY YUEN
192 Lebuh Kimberley, George Town
Tel: 620-137
A long established coffee shop-style restaurant with round marble top tables run by old ladies. *Inexpensive*

TZECHU-LIN VEGETARIAN FOOD CENTRE
229-C Jalan Burmah, George Town
Tel: 373-357
Located diagonally opposite the Buddhist Association of Malaysia. Open from 10am to 9.30pm, serving lunch, fast food, buffets and take aways. *Moderate*

Indian

KALIAMANS
43 Lebuh Penang, George Town
Tel: 628-953
Banana-leaf dining and vegetarian menu available. Opens daily 6am to 10pm and on Sunday from 6pm to 10pm. *Inexpensive*

KASHMIR
105 Jalan Penang, George Town
Tel: 637-411
Naan, tandoori and other North Indian dishes in this basement restaurant. *Moderate*

TANDOORI HOUSE
34-36 Lorong Hutton, George Town
Tel: 619-105
Traditional Mogul and Kashmiri cuisine in the heart of town. *Moderate*

Indian-Muslim

CITY RESTAURANT
85 Lebuh Bishop, George Town
Tel: 617-892
Wide choice of dishes in this *nasi kandar* (mixed food) eatery. *Inexpensive*

DAWOOD
63 Lebuh Queen, George Town
Tel: 611-633, 616-223
Spicy, savoury foods to tempt the palate. Open daily 10am to 9pm. *Moderate*

HAMEEDIA
164-A Lebuh Campbell, George Town
Tel: 611-095
Murtabak, a minced meat or vegetable filled pancake which is the house speciality, is delicious. *Inexpensive*

RESTORAN RAMZAN
48 Lebuh Ah Quee, George Town
Tel: 614-967
A selection of curry dishes to go with steamed white rice. Unpretentious place that opens daily except Sunday. *Inexpensive*

Continental and Western

BACCHUS
1-C Jalan Sungei Kelian
Hillside, Tanjong Bungah
Tel: 802-674, 806-534
Located opposite a hawker centre in a row of shophouses near the 7-Eleven store. Understated bar and restaurant serving good food and wine. Open noon–3pm and from 7–10.30pm daily.
Moderate to Expensive

BRASSERIE
Shangri-La Hotel, Jalan Magazine
Tel: 622-622
Good place for French meals, desserts and imported wines. Sit at tables with red-checked tablecloths. Regular buffet promotions. *Expensive*

D'COTTAGE STEAK INN
160 Jalan Utama, George Town
Tel: 370-887

Western fare prepared by local chefs in casual surroundings. The buffet dinner is quite popular. *Moderate*

LA FARFALLA
Mutiara Beach Resort, Teluk Bahang
Tel: 812-828
Award-winning Italian restaurant with great ambience and excellent food and wines. *Expensive*

MISTRAL
Bayview Beach Resort
Batu Ferringhi
Tel: 812-123
Delicious Mediterranean cuisine. Open daily from 7–11pm. *Expensive*

PEPPINO
Golden Sands Resort, Batu Ferringhi
Tel: 811-911
Freshly-made pizzas, pasta and popular Italian favourites in this trattoria-style eatery. *Expensive*

Japanese

CHIKUYO-TEI
City Bayview Hotel, George Town
Tel: 35-175
Its name translates as 'bamboo pavilion'. Quiet place to have Japanese food in the heart of George Town. *Moderate* to *Expensive*

KAMPACHI
Hotel Equatorial
1 Jalan Bukit Jambul
Tel: 838-111
Located atop the scenic Bukit Jambul near the Bayan Baru and Bayan Lepas industrial parks. Try its Sunday all-you-can-eat buffet lunch. *Expensive*

KURUMAYA
Jalan Burmah, George Town
Tel: 283-222
Unique setting in a former private mansion converted into a restaurant. Ample parking space available if you drive. *Expensive*

THE JAPANESE RESTAURANT
Rasa Sayang Resort, Batu Ferringhi
Tel: 811-811
Fancy eating with private *tatami* rooms and landscaped garden. *Expensive*

TSURU-NO-YA
Mutiara Beach Resort, Teluk Bahang
Tel: 812-828
Exclusive restaurant in a 5-star resort hotel. *Tatami* rooms available on request. *Expensive*

Thai

CAFE D'CHIANGMAI
11 Lintang Burma
Pulau Tikus, George Town
Tel: 372-400/360-022
Chicken with basil leaves, fish with sour mango and green curry are favourites. Open daily for lunch from noon–3pm and dinner from 6–10pm. *Moderate*

THAI PHORNTIP RESTAURANT
1.0.3 Jalan Chan Siew Teong
Tanjung Bungah
Tel: 801-244
Located off Chee Seng Garden near the Hin Bus Company station. Small, cosy place that opens for lunch from 11am–3pm and for dinner from 6–11pm. *Moderate*

YELLOW LIGHT
1-C Jalan Fettes
Tel: 891-471
Prior reservation necessary as only a few tables are available in this garden setting restaurant; walk-in business is discouraged. Daily 7pm to 10.30pm. Closed on Monday. *Expensive*

Antiques and Handicrafts

The range of fine antiques and handicrafts to be found in Penang is extensive. No matter what your interest, taste or budget is, you will find something you like. Ivory-handled Malay *kris* (dagger), silver jewellery, late Ching dynasty ceramics, carved wall panels, Coromandel screens, brass lamps; these and much more await you. Typical Malaysian arts and crafts are pewterware and pottery. Framed specimens of preserved insects like butterflies, scorpions and moths make striking wall decorations. Large painted fans, scroll paintings, decorative paper kites, waxed paper umbrellas, woven mats and all types of baskets are perfect as gifts for family and friends back home.

Browsing is recommended for those with time to spare. For antiques, head for the short stretch of **Jalan Pintal Tali** between Lebuh Kimberley and Jalan Lim Chwee Leong near KOMTAR. One junk shop spreads its wares along the pavement; its interior dusty and crowded. The key-maker shop next door has showcases full of old Chinese porcelain, embroideries and lacquer baskets. Ask to see the main showroom at **Lebuh Hong Kong**. The owner has a house nearby full of larger items like old blackwood furniture sets, wooden sideboards and wardrobes.

The antique shops at **Jalan Penan** are mainly found along the same road, in two locations. The more interesting lies at the head of the road near the Kaliniaga furniture showroom opposite the E & O Hotel; the other is at the junction with Jalan Burmah. The

Batik for sale

former is a shophouse-row full of delightful odds and ends. The latter houses dealers of souvenirs and handicrafts. All the shops sell a mix of real antiquities and modern reproductions and curios. Credit cards are accepted for purchases but discouraged for small, inexpensive items or bargains. Freight forwarding, inclusive of insurance for heavy items, can be easily arranged by these shops.

Several old shops in the centre of **Lebuh Bishop** sell a variety of artifacts and art, furniture and interior decor items like Chinese ceramics, tiny porcelain dolls, antique pocket watches, wall clocks, silver items, jewellery and gilded woodcarvings. Go inside and rummage around for hidden surprises.

The showroom of **Selangor Pewter,** E & O Hotel Arcade, Lebuh Farquhar, Tel: 636-742, makes an interesting visit. Visitors can see a demonstration of basic pewter-making techniques – for instance, how decorative dimples are created on a napkin ring. The range of pewterware comprises beer mugs, tea and coffee sets, clocks, vases, fruit bowls, plates, goblets, letter-openers and many small souvenirs crafted from almost pure tin ore.

Local Snacks

Consider taking home local snacks such as pepper biscuits, bean biscuits, sweetened nutmeg, pickled mango or papaya, prawn crackers, banana chips, salted fish, *durian* cake, spicy *rojak* salad sauce, or else small bottles of clove, nutmeg and linseed oils – all locally produced and much appreciated as presents.

A good place to buy these typical Penang native products and snacks is on the ground floor of **Chowrasta market** in Jalan Penang. The small shops carry a wide variety and most of the edibles are hygienically packed and sealed in plastic packets or in boxes. They are easily portable and suitable as gifts to friends.

The many shops along the steps leading to **Kek Lok Si** temple in Air Itam are also good places to make such purchases. For the last-

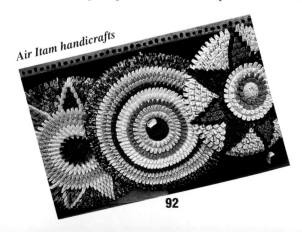

Air Itam handicrafts

minute shopper, a counter at the departure lounge of **Penang International Airport** has similar items for sale, but prices are cheaper downtown.

For the delicious and justifiably famous *tau sar* (mung bean paste) other special biscuits made in Penang, try the following places. You may have to order at least a day or more ahead before you collect them: **Ghee Hiang**, 95 Jalan Pantai, Tel: 620-635; **Him Heang**, 89 Jalan CY Choy, Tel: 613-460; **Hoe Peng**, 434 Jalan Penang, Tel: 372-375; **Lee Hoay Seng**, 1G Jalan Macalister, Tel: 374-458; **Loong Num**, 322 Jalan Penang, Tel: 615-569; **Xiang Phing Bakery**, 4 Jalan Concord 10, Tanjung Bungah, Tel: 802-128.

Batik

Penang *batik* is certainly a good buy either as material or ready-made garments. The cloth on which beeswax designs are printed is usually made of cotton, although silk and synthetic fabrics are widely used too these days. *Batik* is sold by the metre, and ready-to-wear apparel for men, women and children is widely available in many shops.

Locally manufactured *batik* is multi-hued and should be soaked in a solution of common table salt during the first wash. It is advisable to separate *batik* garments from others in the wash as the dyes may run during the first few washes.

Most designs are floral, lending themselves well to bikinis, kaftans, dresses or scarves. Tablecloths, napkins, pareos and shirts in *batik* are also nice reminders of your visit to sunny and colourful Penang island.

For a good idea of prices of *batik* products, look around the big department stores. The government-supervised **Batek Malaysia Berhad** outlet in KOMTAR and many shops in **Jalan Penang** are good for browsing and buying. You will also find lots of colourful *batik* in the tourist shops at **Batu Ferringhi** village and at the factories in **Teluk Bahang**.

Art's Village, located opposite Mutiara Beach Resort at 669 Mukim 2, Teluk Bahang, Tel: 811-679, has a gallery showing original *batik* paintings by local artists. **Craft Batik Sdn Bhd**, 651 Mukim 2, Teluk Bahang, Tel: 811-302 is a factory and showroom displaying *batik* fabrics and ready-made clothing.

Yahong Art Gallery, 58-D Batu Ferringhi, Tel: 811-251, is a large shop specialising in arts and crafts but with an emphasis on *batik*. The gallery is owned by the Chuah family of artists, renowned for their fine *batik* art works. Their *batik* paintings grace many private art collections and several of their designs have been used on UNESCO greeting cards.

Jewellery

Lebuh Campbell, near the Kapitan Kling Mosque, has numerous goldsmiths and jewellers. These shops are frequented by local residents before major festivals like Chinese New Year and the Muslim

Hari Raya, or when the price of gold plunges steeply from time to time. These shops may look daunting to the visitor as they usually have gun-toting security guards outside to protect them; but don't worry, they are there for your protection.

To view locally manufactured jewellery made for export, visit the **OG Design Sdn Bhd** factory and showroom at the Free Trade Zone 3 in Bayan Lepas, Tel: 832-011. Free transport is provided from your hotel on request for a guided tour of this German-run jewellery manufacturer on weekdays only. The same company also has a jewellery showroom at the shopping arcade of the Golden Sands Resort in Batu Ferringhi, Tel: 812-323, which opens daily from 9am to 7pm.

Department Stores

For easy and convenient one-stop shopping under one roof, KOMTAR is recommended as there are about 300 retail outlets, including two big departmental stores, inside this huge shopping complex. Both **Super KOMTAR** and **Yaohan,** a Japanese-owned and run megastore, have a wide range of consumer products should you require cosmetics, fragrances, baggage, clothing, footwear, sporting goods and other items.

Nearby, at the intersection of Jalan Penang, Jalan Datuk Keramat and Jalan Brick Kiln is GAMA, another large, multi-storey department store which is part of the international Japanese Sogo group.

Along busy Jalan Burmah is **Super Burma**, sited between Jalan Madras and Jalan Rangoon. About 200m (220yds) away is **Penang Plaza**, a shopping mall with a large supermarket, boutiques, hair styling salons, computer outlets, a pharmacy, healthfood store, jewellers and a toy shop. The **Axis Complex** at the junction with Jalan Cantonment in the Pulau Tikus area, has the Plus Zone supermarket and many stores within.

There are several other department stores in Penang which may be more accessible depending on where you are staying. For the inveterate shopper, rest assured that there will be lots of bargains wherever you look.

Cookies at Pulau Tikus market

Calendar of Special Events

The multi-racial, multi-religious population ensures a calendar filled with festivals every month. Although you may not plan your visit around these celebrations, many of the colourful festivals provide the opportunity for some great photography, if you're there at the right time.

Exact dates of some Chinese, Muslim and Hindu festivals vary from year to year, so be sure to check the local calendar or with the tourist information office.

JANUARY/FEBRUARY

New Year's Day. 1 January. A public and banking holiday.

Thaipusam. A Hindu festival in honour of Lord Subramaniam, characterised by devotees piercing their bodies with sharp spikes as penance. Devotees also carry *kavadis*, huge arched structures, and take part in a street procession.

These *kavadis* are held in place by hooks and skewers which pierce the body. Strangely though, not a drop of blood is shed as the devotees go into a trance-like state. They would also have spent months of prayer and fasting to prepare for this day.

Chinese New Year. The dates of this festival are set according to the

Incense and paper money for the Hungry Ghost Festival

lunar calendar, but normally fall within the first two months of the year. Two public holidays are set aside for the occasion, although the entire celebration runs for 15 days. The sizeable Penang Chinese community prepares for this event by spring-cleaning their homes and baking various types of sweets and savouries weeks before the first day of the Chinese New Year.

A traditional practice is for the older (and normally, married) Chi-

96

nese to give the younger ones red packets containing money, called *ang pows*.

The 15th or last day of Chinese New Year is known as *Chap Goh Meh*. Shopkeepers burn giant joss-sticks on this day. A *Peranakan dondang sayang* band sings nostalgic songs to serenade the public in a bus decked up for the night.

Birthday of the Jade Emperor or God of Heaven. Corresponds with the ninth day of the Chinese first lunar month. Pilgrims hike up to the **Cave Temple** near the Hill Railway in Air Itam.

FEBRUARY

The Birthday of the Deity Chor Soo Kong. Held twice a year, the second occasion in July/August. Again, precise dates vary from year to year, since it is fixed by the lunar calendar. This celebration is observed with devotees congregating at the **Snake Temple** to offer prayers, incense and eggs to the god, Chor Soo Kong.

FEBRUARY/MARCH

Birthday of Tua Pek Kong or God of Prosperity. Celebrated at the **Tanjung Tokong Temple** which is dedicated to this deity. Chinese opera shows are staged in the vicinity of the temple.

MARCH/APRIL

Birthday of the Goddess of Mercy (Kuan Yin). This takes place again in July and October. Devotees flock to the temple at **Pitt Street**, built in honour of Kuan Yin.

Cheng Beng. The Chinese version of All Souls Day, when descendants visit the tombs of their dead ances-tors to pay respect and pray for the souls of the dead.

APRIL

Songkran or Water Festival. The Thai water festival celebrated by the Thai community in Penang. Participate in the festival at the Burmese Temple in Burma Lane or Perak Road. Decorative paper boats are made and released into the sea at Gurney Drive in the evening.

Tamil New Year. Malaysians of Indian descent wake early, take oil baths, dress in new clothes and visit Hindu temples for prayers on *Varusha Pirapu*.

Easter Sunday. Christians celebrate in church; hotels celebrate with bunnies and egg hunts; hot-cross buns and chocolate eggs sold widely.

Vasakhi. This is the New Year of the Sikhs. Sikhs read their holy book, *Granth Sahib*, non-stop for two days before the final celebrations at their Jalan Brick Kiln temple, called Gurdwara.

MAY/JUNE

Vesak Day. Celebrated in commemoration of Buddha's birthday, enlightenment and achievement of *Nirvana*, marked by a procession of the statue of Buddha through the main roads of the city.

Penang MAS Dragon International Boat Festival. An annual affair of the battle of the 'dragons'. Local and international dragon boat teams pit their strengths in the fight for supremacy.

JUNE

The Chung Festival. Also known as the Dragon Boat Festival, it commemorates an ancient Chinese legend; the unsuccessful attempt to save the poet, Chu Yuan, who drowned himself to protest against corruption in the emperor's court.

In an attempt to save him, fishermen threw glutinous rice dumplings, *chung*, into the river to feed the fishes and prevent his body from being eaten by them.

JULY

Birthday of TYT Yang Di-Pertua Negeri. The people of Penang celebrate the official birthday of HE The Governor with parades and prayers. Buildings are gaily decorated for the occasion.
St Anne's Feast. Celebrated at **St Anne's Church** at Bukit Mertajam

with prayers lasting nine days. Street candle light processions take place on July 26 and 29.

AUGUST

Hungry Ghost Festival. A month-long festival during which the 'hungry ghosts' are temporarily released from hell to the realm of the living. Sumptuous offerings, especially by the market stall-holders, are made to placate the ghosts. Chinese opera and puppet shows are staged at the main markets in Penang.
Festival of the Seven Sisters. Prayers and offerings of food are made to the Weaving Maiden while unmarried Chinese maidens pray to her for good husbands.
Malaysia's National Day Celebrations. A big parade is held at the Esplanade in the morning of this public holiday.

AUGUST/SEPTEMBER

Moon Cake Festival. The overthrow of the tyrannical Mongol overlords in ancient China is commemorated

Chinese opera adds to the riotous attempts to placate the spirits

Offerings for hungry ghosts at Lorong Stewart

by the Chinese. Historically, a festival for poets, women and children.

OCTOBER

MAS International Marathon. Penang's premier sports event, attracting a crowd of over 8,000, including top world runners.

Kew Ong Yeah or **Festival of the Nine Emperor Gods**. Fire-walking ceremonies, and mediums in trance perform various feats at dusk outside the Chinese temple at **Jalan Magazine**, **Jalan Burma** and **Jalan Noordin** over nine days. Pilgrims climb the 1,200 steps to the Taoist temple of **Ching Kuan Ssu** at Paya Terubong hill. The **Kuan Yin Teng Temple** in Jalan Burma has many vegetarian stalls during the festival.

World Formula I Powerboat Championship. A heart-stopping event with some of the world's fastest racers competing.

OCTOBER/NOVEMBER

Deepavali. This Hindu festival commemorates the slaying of the tyrant demon king Narageswaran by Lord Krishna. It literally means 'rows of lights' as oil lamps are lit to brighten homes. Devotees offer items like flowers, betelnut, betel leaves, limes, incense and coins in half a coconut shell.

After an oil bath at dawn, women wear new *saris* and men *dhotis* for prayers. Children beg forgiveness and seek blessings from elders. Sweetmeats and cakes are offered to relatives and friends.

NOVEMBER

Star Walk. Annual event attracting an average of 10,000 participants from Malaysia and Singapore.

Loy Krathong. The Thai community meet at the **Wat Chaiya Mangkalaram** and proceed to **Pesiaran Gurney** where they send floral and leaf floats adrift on the sea at this evocative celebration. This offering to water spirits signifies the passage of sins and misdeeds and is a time of atonement. The leaf cups or *krathongs* bear lit candles, joss sticks and flowers.

Pesta Pulau Pinang. Trade and Industrial fair lasting the whole month, providing visitors with some of the best aspects of cultural and recreational activities.

DECEMBER

Penang Grand Prix. An annual event organised by the Penang State Government where saloon cars and motorcycles race along the street circuit of Penang.

Christmas. Churches are packed on Christmas Eve; carolling on the streets. Hotels and restaurants serve traditional Christmas fare. Christian families throw open houses for relatives and friends.

Chingay. A grand parade when giant triangular flagpoles are held aloft and carried through the streets. The carnival-like atmosphere is enhanced by lion dancers and musicians. The flag bearers perform acrobatics by balancing 10-m (33-ft) high poles on foreheads, shoulders, stomachs, and even in their mouths. A spectacle not to be missed. Ringside seats are free along the route of the procession. Try not to be late or you may end up standing throughout the whole parade.

New Year's Eve. End-of-year revelry best enjoyed in hotels, pubs and discos. Avoid driving before and after midnight as the streets get choked with vehicles. Ships in the harbour blast their horns and cars do likewise on the streets. The night gets wild and frenzied at Pesiaran Gurney.

*Variable dates: Muslim festivals fall on a different month every year so be sure that you check the local calendar.

Awal Ramadan. The dates of this is determined each year by the Prime Minister's department. This is the start of the Muslim fasting month when most Muslim-run food establishments will close for business.

Hari Raya Puasa. It marks the end of the fasting month of *Ramadan*, when Muslim houses are thrown open to relatives and friends.

Hari Raya Haji. A religious day for Muslims, marking the 10th day of the 12th moon of the Muslim Calendar, when pilgrims in Mecca visit the *Baitullah* (Black Stone) in the last phase of the *Haj*.

Prophet Mohammad's Birthday. It is observed by Muslims who celebrate the birthday of *Nabi Muhammad*, born in 571AD. They congregate to offer prayers of praise at mosques. Eminent Islamic scholars are often invited to give talks. This is a national public holiday. A procession is held in George Town, and the faithful recite verses from the *Quran* during the march. Only menfolk may take part, and they carry cloth banners inscribed with verses from the *Quran*.

Practical Information

GETTING THERE

By Air

Penang International Airport is 16km (10 miles) from George Town and 36km (22½ miles) from Batu Ferringhi. It is serviced by five major carriers: Cathay Pacific, Eva Air, Malaysia Airlines, Singapore Airlines and Thai International. By air, Penang is 40 minutes from Kuala Lumpur, the Malaysian capital; 65 minutes from Singapore; one hour and 45 minutes from Bangkok; three hours from Hong Kong.

TRAVEL ESSENTIALS

Climate/When to Visit

One of the 13 states in the Federation of Malaysia, Penang enjoys a warm and humid equatorial climate all year around. The temperature hovers between 23°C and 32°C (75°F to 95°F) without seasonal changes. The mean annual rainfall is about 267cm (105 inches) through-out the year, with September to November being the wettest months. So any time is a good time to visit.

Clothing

Light cotton clothes are ideal in this balmy tropical weather. Shorts and T-shirts are perfect for most of your sightseeing. When visiting mosques though, make sure that the legs are covered to the knees. This is a Muslim country and so topless sunbathing is frowned upon at the beaches. Slather yourself with a good sunblock, especially at the beach and drink lots of fluids to guard againt dehydration.

Passports

Visitors need a valid passport or an internationally recognised travel document. A disembarkation card must be completed and handed to the Immigration Officer on arrival. Passports or other recognised travel documents are also necessary for travel between Peninsular Malaysia and the East Malaysian states of Sabah and Sarawak. All passports should be valid for at least six months beyond the date of their expiry.

Visas

No visas are required for citizens of Commonwealth countries – except citizens of Bangladesh, India, Pakistan and Sri Lanka – British protected nationals, citizens of the Republic of Ireland, Singapore, Brunei, Lichtenstein, the Netherlands, San Marino and Switzerland.

For visits not exceeding three months, no visas are required for citizens of Algeria, Austria, Bahrain, Belgium, Czechoslovakia, Denmark, Egypt, Finland, France, Germany, Iceland, Italy, Japan, Jordan, Kuwait, Lebanon, Luxembourg, Morocco, North Yemen, Norway, Oman, South Korea, Sweden, Tunisia, Turkey, United Arab Emirates and the United States.

A one-month visa-free stay is permitted for citizens of ASEAN countries and citizens of Argentina, Angola, Bhutan, Bolivia, Benin, Brazil, Burundi, Cameroon, Chad, Chile, Colombia, Congo, Corsica, Costa Rica, Dominican Republic, Ecuador, El Salvador, Gabon, Greenland, Greece, Guam, Guatemala, Guinea, Hungary, Kampuchea, Laos, Myanmar and Poland.

Vaccinations

No cholera or smallpox vaccination is required except for visitors from infected areas of yellow fever endemic zones.

Airport Tax

The domestic airport tax is RM5 while that for international flights is RM20.

Customs

Dutiable goods should be declared. Penang's Bayan Lepas International Airport has a green lane for visitors without dutiable items.

Duty-free Goods

A wide variety of duty-free items such as liquors, liqueurs, cigarettes, tobacco and cigars are available from duty-free shops. Non-dutiable goods include: cigarette lighters, perfumes, skincare products, clocks and watches, ballpoint and fountain pens, fashion leather goods, sportswear, cameras, radios and pocket calculators.

Note that taped video cassettes require customs clearance, and the export of antiquities is subject to the provisions of the Antiquities Act.

Quarantine

All animals or pets brought into Penang will be quarantined and require health certificates issued in the country of origin. Visitors must declare to customs or the quarantine inspector of any plant or parts of a plant in their possession, and of their visit to any country in South America and the Caribbean during the last 30 days.

Electricity

Power supply is 220 or 240 volts at 50Hz. Most outlets use a three-pin, flat-pronged plug. Equipment using 110 volts will require a transformer.

Time Differences

Penang is eight hours ahead of Greenwich Mean Time (GMT) and 16 hours ahead of US Pacific Standard Time.

Geography

Penang island, about 5° from the equator, lies off the northwest coast of Peninsular Malaysia. It is 285sq km (110sq miles) in area.

Population

About one million multi-racial people live in Penang. The urban centre is George Town, founded in 1786.

Culture and Languages

The customs, religions and language

View from KOMTAR Tower: the port and mainland

of many nations converge in Malaysia.

The official language is Malay; English is almost as widely-used, but mostly in business and trade. Mandarin and Chinese dialects (Cantonese, Hakka, Hokkien); Thai; Tamil and other Indian dialects (Bengali, Hindu Malayalam, Punjabi and Telegu) are spoken.

Religion

Freedom of worship exists, with Islam being the state religion. Muslim mosques, Buddhist and Hindu temples and Christian churches are commonly found throughout the island. Religious festivals are celebrated regularly all through the year.

Currency

The basic unit of currency is the Ringgit Malaysia (RM). It is issued in RM1, RM5, RM10, RM20, RM50, RM100, RM500 and RM1,000 notes. Coins are in denominations of 1 sen, 5 sen, 10 sen, 50 sen and RM1.

Useful for telephones and parking meters are the 10 sen, 20 sen, 50 sen and RM1 coins.

At time of press, US$1 buys RM2.56. The prevailing exchange rates of major currencies are posted daily in all banks, listed in newspapers and displayed at many hotels.

Banks

Banking hours are from 10am to 3pm Monday–Friday; 9.30am to 11.30am on Saturday.

The main banking district is Lebuh Pantai in George Town. Penang is well represented by banking groups like Citibank, Hongkong Bank, Standard Chartered Bank and ABN-AMRO Bank.

Money Changers

Major foreign currencies are easily exchanged in banks and by money changers. Big stores and some touristy outlets are prepared to accept cash like US dollars and sterling pounds as payment.

Look for licensed money changers; they operate from 8.30am to 7pm. Their exchange rates are displayed on a whiteboard and are usually slightly better than those at the banks.

Credit Card Facilities

Credit cards such as American Express, Diners, MasterCard, Visa and JCB International are accepted in leading hotels, restaurants, car

rental agencies, travel agencies and department stores.

Travellers' cheques

Internationally recognised travellers' cheques like American Express and Thomas Cook are widely accepted and may be cashed at commercial banks. Most money changers, however, are reluctant to accept them without proper documentation and will record passport information and other details.

Euro Cheques

Local banks in Penang need clearance from the issuing banks. Normally, Euro Cheques can be transacted quickly in branches of European-based banks.

Tipping

Though not a local custom, many locals practise tipping in recognition of good service. In restaurants and hotels, most bills include a 10 percent service charge already. Give what you think is fair. For trishaw and taxi rides, feel free to pay the exact fare or ask the driver to keep the change.

Tourist Information

PENANG TOURIST CENTRE
Penang Port Commission Building, Ground Floor Arcade, Pesara King Edward. Tel/Fax: 616-663 for further information about Penang. Hours: 8.30am–4.30pm Monday–Friday (lunch hour: closed from 1pm–2pm); 8.30am–1pm Saturday. Closed on Sunday and public holidays.

MALAYSIAN TOURISM PROMOTION BOARD (MTPB)
At Jalan Tun Syed Sheh Barakbah behind the clock tower opposite the east wall of Fort Cornwallis. The MTPB also has a counter at the airport providing information on Malaysia at Tel: 619-067. Opening hours are the same as the Penang Tourist Centre except on Friday when the lunch hour is from 12.15pm–2.45pm. Closed on Sunday and public holidays.

TOURIST INFORMATION CENTRE
Managed by the Penang Tourist Guides Association and situated at 3rd level, Concourse area, KOMTAR, Jalan Penang. Tel: 614-461. Qualified and registered foreign language tour guides can be booked at the counter. Opening hours: 10am–8pm Monday to Sunday.

HOURS AND HOLIDAYS

Business Hours

Business hours for shops are from 10am to 10pm daily. Government offices open from 8.15am to 4.15pm weekdays; 8.15am to 1 pm on Saturday. Lunch break is from 12.45pm to 2pm. On Friday, lunchtime is from 12.15pm to 2.45pm. Commercial hours for private companies are from 9am to 5pm on weekdays; 9am to 1pm on Saturday.

Public Holidays

New Year's Day: January 1
Chinese New Year: January
Thaipusam: January/February
Labour Day: May 1
Vesak Day: May/June

HM The King's Birthday: June 5
Governor's Birthday: July 10
National Day: August 31
Deepavali: October/November
Christmas Day: December 25

The dates of Muslim holidays like the following are determined by an Islamic calendar:
Hari Raya Puasa
Hari Raya Haji
Maal Hijrah Awal Muharram
Prophet Mohammad's Birthday

GETTING AROUND

Convenient modes of transportation are available. Public transport include public buses, taxis and trishaws. You can also rent a car, motorcycle or bicycle easily. Rental of cars start from RM100 per day inclusive of insurance.

Taxis

Taxi hire charges are about RM20 an hour or RM120 a day. Where meters are not used, negotiate with the driver on an agreed fare before boarding. You could also ask your hotel receptionist for a price estimate of the ride to your destination.

Limousine taxis are air-conditioned, chauffeur-driven cars which can be hired for about RM30 per hour, for a minimum of three hours. Your hotel should be able to arrange for one.

Trishaws

A novel way to travel around in if you have the time. The three-wheeled vehicle can carry one to two passengers comfortably and is recommended for short journeys. It gives a good view of the city in slow motion as you are driven by leg power. Trishaws cost about RM8 per hour for hire. A ride of about

1½km (1 mile) will cost about RM4. It is advisable to agree on a fare before boarding.

Car Rental

AVIS RENT-A-CAR
388 Batu Ferringhi, Tel: 811-522
Bayan Lepas Airport, Tel: 839-633

BUDGET RENT-A-CAR
105-A Ground floor,
Oriental Hotel Building,
Jalan Penang, Tel: 631-240
Bayan Lepas Airport, Tel: 838-891
Reservations, (toll-free) 800-3191

HERTZ RENT-A-CAR
38 Lebuh Farquhar,
Tel: 635-914/638-602
Bayan Lepas Airport, Tel: 830-208

ACCOMMODATION

Penang has well over 8,000 rooms of different categories. The Penang Tourist Centre (Tel: 616-663) provides information on lodging. At the airport, the major hotels have booking and reservations counters to assist arriving passengers. It is best to reserve your room in advance, especially during the busy peak periods of Malaysian school vacations, local festivals and year-end holidays.

The chief tourist hub is the north coast area of Batu Ferringhi. George Town has its share of modern, deluxe hotels. Generally, a wide range of accommodation is available to suit all budgets. All room rates are subject to 10 percent service charge and 5 percent government tax.

An approximate guide to current room rates for a standard double room inclusive of local taxes is as follows: $=less than RM50; $$= RM50-RM100; $$$=Rm100-RM200; $$$=RM200-RM300; $$$$=more than RM300.

Beach Hotels

BAYVIEW BEACH RESORT
Batu Ferringhi
Tel: 812-123
Sea-fronting hotel with 426 rooms and suites. Previous winner of the Tourism Gold Award for the best first class hotel. *$$$$*

CASUARINA BEACH HOTEL
Batu Ferringhi
Tel: 811-711
All 180 sea view rooms have their own balconies. *$$$*

CROWN PRINCE
Tanjung Bungah
Tel: 804-111
Sea-facing hotel with 280 rooms, each with its own balcony. A 9-hole putting green is located right in front of the hotel lobby entrance. Sea and land recreational activities can be arranged *$$$*

FERRINGHI BEACH HOTEL
Batu Ferringhi
Tel: 805-999
Spacious, airy hotel with 350 rooms facing the sea which is across the road and accessible by a covered overhead bridge. *$$$*

GOLDEN SANDS RESORT
Batu Ferringhi
Tel: 811-911
A 310-room hotel well-known for its high standards of service and fun-filled activities all year round. Watersports centre and kiddie club. Free shuttle service to town and back daily. *$$$$*

HOLIDAY INN
Batu Ferringhi
Tel: 811-601
350-room hotel with a tower extension across the road linked by an overhead bridge. *$$$$*

LONE PINE HOTEL
Batu Ferringhi
Tel: 811-511
Small hotel with family and economy rooms and pool along a busy stretch of beach. *$$*

MAR VISTA RESORT
1 Jalan Batu Ferringhi
Tel: 803-388
Hillside hotel complex comprising a clubhouse, three low-rise and two high-rise buildings with private apartments. *$$$*

MOTEL SRI PANTAI
516-G Jalan Hashim
Tanjung Bungah
Tel: 895-566
Modest 20-room hotel just off the main road but on the beach next to the Chinese Swimming Club. *$$*

MUTIARA BEACH RESORT
Teluk Bahang
Tel: 812-828
Sprawling, deluxe, 440-room beach

resort with top class facilities and amenities on an 18-acre site. Chinese, Japanese, Italian restaurants and a 24-hour coffee house. *$$$$*

NOVOTEL PENANG
Tanjung Bungah
Tel: 803-333

Has its own private, secluded beach with watersports only 10 minutes from town. Health and recreational centre for fitness and sports enthusiasts. Free shuttle bus downtown and back. *$$$$*

PENANG PARKROYAL
Batu Ferringhi
Tel: 811-113
A 333-room beachfront hotel with swim-up bar at its pool. Watersports equipment include catamarans, water-skis and windsurf boards. *$$$*

RASA SAYANG RESORT
Batu Ferringhi
Tel: 811-811
A 500-room seaside hotel with huge grounds, seasports, recreational facilities, restaurants and disco. Its new deluxe wing offers world class services. Complimentary coach shuttle from resort to town. *$$$$*

George Town

CITY BAYVIEW HOTEL
Lebuh Farquhar
Tel: 633-161
Located in the charming historic district and has the island's only revolving restaurant on its top floor. Its reasonably-priced Eliza outlet is reputed to be the best Malay restaurant in the country. *$$$*

E & O HOTEL
Lebuh Farquhar
Tel: 630-630
Penang's grande dame, built over 100 years ago by the Sarkies brothers who also erected the Raffles Hotel in Singapore and the Strand Hotel in Yangon (Myanmar). Old, colonial style recapturing bygone era. *$$$*

HOTEL EQUATORIAL
1 Jalan Bukit Jambul
Tel: 838-000
Large convention hotel sited next to 18-hole designer golf course; near factories in free trade zone and 10 minutes from the airport. *$$$$*

SHANGRI-LA HOTEL
Jalan Magazine
Tel: 622-622
Part of the sprawling KOMTAR complex, right in the city centre near shops, business and government offices. Provides free regular shuttle to affiliated beach hotels and back. *$$$$*

COMMUNICATIONS AND NEWS

Telecommunications
Cables, telexes and faxes may be sent through Telegraph Offices at the following places:

BANGUNAN TUANKU SYED PUTRA
Lebuh Downing,
Tel: 610-791
24-hour service.

KEDAI TELEKOM
1st Floor, Jalan Burmah,
Tel: 373-273
24-hour service.

PENANG INTERNATIONAL AIRPORT
Tel: 834-411
Hours: 8.30 am to 9.30 pm.

Most big hotels also offer telex and fax facilities, and IDD phones. To call abroad directly, first dial the international access code, 60, followed by the country code. If using a US credit phone card, dial the company's access number: Sprint, Tel: 800-0018; AT&T, Tel: 800-0011; MCI, Tel: 800-0012. For assistance, dial 108 for the overseas operator. The area code for Penang is 04 if calling within Malaysia. Additional information for local calls are obtainable from any telephone directory.

Calls at public telephone booths cost 10 sen minimum. Phonecards and credit cards are accepted at designated public phone booths.

Media

The English language dailies are *The New Straits Times* (morning paper), *The Star* (morning paper) and the *Malay Mail* (afternoon paper). You can also get regional and international newspapers such as the *International Herald Tribune* and *Asian Wall Street Journal* from news vendors and hotel bookstores.

Radio Malaysia broadcasts in the four major languages of English, Chinese, Malay and Tamil. Check the dailies for broadcasting schedules of the English-language programmes.

There are four television channels, namely TV1, TV2, TV3 and TV4, which feature a wide variety of programmes in the four main languages. Again, check the dailies for programme schedules. Most international class hotels have their own in-house video programmes.

Public Clinics/ Hospitals

Government clinics charge a basic fee of RM1. A consultancy fee is required when a specialist is requested.

GENERAL HOSPITAL
Jalan Hospital, Tel: 373-333

BUKIT MERTAJAM DISTRICT HOSPITAL
Tel: 513-333

Private Clinics/Hospitals

Be prepared to pay a lot for personalised medical attention and specialist consultancy at private clinics and hospitals. Most top hotels can provide emergency medical aid from doctors on call 24 hours a day.

GLENEAGLES MEDICAL CENTRE
1 Jalan Pangkor, Tel: 376-111

PENANG ADVENTIST HOSPITAL
465 Jalan Burmah, Tel: 373-344

Many hotels have swimming pools. Tennis and squash courts, bowling alleys, snooker centres, golf courses and other recreational facilities are also available. Horse racing is held during weekends. Hill climbs, mass jogs, long-distance running, water-skiing, windsurfing, para-sailing, boating and fishing are popular. Modern fitness centres and health clubs are found at large hotels.

Golf Courses

BUKIT JAMBUL COUNTRY CLUB
2 Jalan Bukit Jambul
Tel: 842-255
A challenging, international-class championship course designed by Robert Trent Jones Jr. The par-72, 18-hole, 5,588m layout offers exciting play and good views of the Penang coastline.

BUKIT JAWI GOLF RESORT
6591 Main Road, Sungai Bakap
14200 Seberang Perai Selatan
Tel: 522-612, 522-613

AIR FORCE GOLF CLUB
Tentera Udara DiRaja Malaysia

12990 Butterworth
Tel: 322-632
A 9-hole, par-34, 2,634m layout on the peninsula mainland opposite Penang island.

PENANG TURF CLUB GOLF SECTION
Jalan Batu Gantong, 10450 Penang
Tel: 376-701
This par-72, 18-hole course has seven holes on the racetrack.

Museums and Art Galleries
PENANG STATE MUSEUM AND ART GALLERY
Lebuh Farquhar
Tel: 613-144
Neolithic adzes, cultural dioramas, antique furniture and porcelain, the Tunku Abdul Rahman collection of hand-held weapons, old colonial paintings, natural history, embroideries and costumes, pre-war artifacts and relics. Open 9am–5pm daily; closed between 12.15–2.45pm on Friday.

UNIVERSITI SAINS MALAYSIA
Museum and Art Gallery
Minden (near Penang Bridge)
Tel: 877-888
Collections of modern Malaysian art, Southeast Asian ceramics, ethnic textiles, antique jewellery and native crafts. Open 10am to 5pm weekdays; closed weekends.

YAHONG ART GALLERY
58-D Batu Ferringhi
Tel: 811-251
Private collection of the Chuah family batik paintings, arts and handicrafts, antiques and jewellery. Open daily from 9am to 7pm.

THE ART GALLERY
7 Jalan Gottlieb
Tel: 368-219
An artists' agent and dealer open

from 9.30am to 6pm from Tuesday to Sunday, closed on Monday.

USEFUL ADDRESSES
Foreign Missions
Please note that foreign missions open only from 9am to 12 noon for visa applications. Closed on weekends and public holidays.

THE BANGLADESH CONSULATE
15 Lebuh Bishop
Tel: 621-085/616-296/628-236

BRITISH REPRESENTATIVE, ROYAL NORWEGIAN CONSULATE AND SWEDISH CONSULATE
c/o Plantation Agency Sdn Bhd
Standard Chartered Bank Chambers
2 Lebuh Pantai
Tel: 625-333

CONSULATE GENERAL OF JAPAN
2 Jalan Biggs
Tel: 368-222

HON. CONSULATE OF THE FEDERAL REPUBLIC OF GERMANY
Robert Bosch (M) Sdn Bhd
Bayan Lepas Free Trade Zone
Tel: 838-340

HON. FRENCH CONSULATE
Wisma Rajab, 82 Lebuh Bishop
Tel: 629-707

INDONESIAN CONSULATE
467 Jalan Burmah
Tel: 374-686, 374-704

NETHERLANDS CONSULATE CHANCERY
ABN-AMRO Bank
9 Lebuh Pantai
Tel: 622-144

ROYAL DANISH CONSULATE
Bernam Agencies, 3rd Floor
Hongkong Bank Chambers

Lebuh Downing
Tel: 624-88

ROYAL THAI CONSULATE-GENERAL
1 Jalan Tunku Abdul Rahman
Tel: 378-029

TURKISH CONSULATE
7 Pengkalan Weld
Tel: 615-933/615-934

USEFUL TELEPHONE NUMBERS

Tourist Police, Tel: 615-522
(George Town); 811-434 **(Batu Ferringhi)**.
Police, Fire Brigade and Ambulance, Tel: 999
Customs Department, Tel: 622-300
General Post Office, Tel: 618-973
Government Information Office, Tel: 616-677
Immigration Department, Tel: 615-122
Malayan Railway, Tel: 610-290
Penang Hill Railway, Tel: 683-263

Airlines
Penang International Airport, Tel: 834-411
Air Canada, Tel: 623-615
Air France, Tel: 622-605
British Airways, Tel: 616-342
Cathay Pacific Airways, Tel: 620-411/610-815
China Airlines, Tel: 627-091
Eva Air, Tel: 631-484
Japan Airlines, Tel: 620-590
KLM **Royal Dutch Airlines**, Tel: 378-046
Malaysia Airlines,Tel: 830-811 **(Airport Counter)**; Tel: 620-011 (KOMTAR)
Northwest Orient Airlines, Tel: 619-563/615-827
Pelangi Air, Tel: 620-011
Singapore Airlines, Tel: 363-201
Thai Airways International, Tel: 366-233

Cover and backcover Ingo Jezierski (Apa Photo)
Photography Ingo Jezierski *and*
Pages 6/7 Manfred Gottschalk (Apa Photo)
10/11 Philip Little (Apa Photo)

Project Editors Ilsa Sharp *and* Yeow Mei Sin
Handwriting V Rarl
Cartography Berndtson & Berndtson
Cover Design Klaus Geisler

INSIGHT *pocket* GUIDES

• •

United States: **Houghton Mifflin Company, Boston MA 02108**
Tel: (800) 2253362 Fax: (800) 4589501

Canada: **Thomas Allen & Son, 390 Steelcase Road East**
Markham, Ontario L3R 1G2
Tel: (416) 4759126 Fax: (416) 4756747

Great Britain: **GeoCenter IIK, Hampshire RG22 4BJ**
Tel: (256) 817987 Fax: (256) 817988

Worldwide: **Höfer Communications Singapore 2262**
Tel: (65) 8612755 Fax: (65) 8616438

❝ I was first drawn to the Insight Guides by the excellent "Nepal" volume. I can think of no book which so effectively captures the essence of a country. Out of these pages leaped the Nepal I know – the captivating charm of a people and their culture. I've since discovered and enjoyed the entire Insight Guide Series. Each volume deals with a country or city in the same sensitive depth, which is nowhere more evident than in the superb photography. ❞

Sir Edmund Hillary

INSIGHT GUIDES

COLORSET NUMBERS